Owning
Poverty
A Transformational Journey

ISBN: 978-168-61-1999-6

For details on supplemental resources contact the
author at the book's website
www.owningpoverty.com

PREFACE

This project started with some questions: "If we desire to witness to and participate in Christ's Kingdom transformation, what needs to be transformed in us first?" "What changes in our values and attitudes are prerequisite in service to the Good News to the poor?" "How can we gain a Kingdom posture of: humility, openness, engagement, faith, discernment, discipline, cultural awareness, creativity, community, hope, solidarity, ownership, freedom from fear, commitment, love, etc.?" Resisting the tendency to avoid painful realities, we must approach vulnerability, in vulnerability. We will need to bring our whole persons in order to understand the whole truth about poverty in ourselves and others.

Exiting our comfort zone into new contexts is one way to gain a deeper understanding of poverty, enabling us to experience first-hand, God's transformation of different communities and individuals. I have seen people in cross-cultural contexts see poverties they could not see at home, choose a "posture of poverty" which God calls blessed, and grow in their affinity with God's heart for the poor. There is great potential in such intentional responses to God's call to GO, not in a spirit of rescuing, pretending we are above the poor, but going where God can meet us in our poverty.[1]

To this end, the GO ED. semester study abroad program was created to transform the next generation to own and end poverty. Through the structure of a university credit-bearing, cross-cultural, service learning experience in developing contexts, the program engaged the hands, heads, and hearts of hundreds of young people. Early on we realized we needed a guided Christian spiritual formation curriculum to process the encounter with poverty together. This is how *Owning Poverty* was born.[2]

Subsequently, *Owning Poverty* was shaped and reshaped over a decade by the issues at the intersect of observed and experienced human poverties, raw poverties like genocide and human trafficking, as well as less visible ones. GO ED. students, staff and alumni have raised and deeply engaged the questions that became the themes and chapters of

---

[1] This work owes a deep debt to the following advocates of biblical theology of poverty. Myers, Bryant L. *Walking with the Poor: Principles and Practices of Transformational Development* (New York: World Vision/ Orbis Books,1999). Sider, Ronald J. *Rich Christians in an Age of Hunger* 2nd ed. (London: Hodder, 1997). Christian, Jayakumar *God of the Empty-Handed: Poverty, Power & the Kingdom of God* (Monrovia: MARC, 1999). Wolterstorff, Nicolas *Until Justice and Peace Embrace: the Kuyper Lectures for 1981* (Amsterdam: Eerdmans, 1983). Stott, John, *Issues Facing Christians Today* (London:(Marshall Pickering,1990). Sugden, Chris *Gospel, Culture, and Transformation* (Oxford: Regnum, 2000).

[2] Some of the foundational owning poverty concepts were explored in Pucci, Michael S. "The Gospel and Human Poverty", in *Hearts Aflame*, Ed. Michael Tan (Singapore: Genesis Books, 2008). Scripture versions quoted in the text (chiefly KJV) are from www.biblegateway.com.

this book. The hours of prayerful preparation time by facilitators and honest enquiry from participants has created the ethos in which a journey of this kind is even possible. The content was also refined in the context of professional graduate courses I taught for Regent College, Eastern University, and Multnomah University.

I am grateful for the integrity with which we (as an epistemic community) have engaged and attempted to internalize and incarnate in meaningful lives, these difficult biblical realities encountered in *Owning Poverty*. It is this desire, to see God change the world, and the willingness to invite him to begin with us, which has created both this content and community, that continues to serve as a catalyst for ongoing Kingdom transformation.

I also gratefully acknowledge the advocacy and support of the organizations who have shared in the vision of *Owning Poverty* and who have extended its use as a tool for guiding mutual transformation in staff development and higher education for service among the world's most vulnerable people: Rural Care Foundation, Food for the Hungry, Word Made Flesh, Freedom Resource International, InterVarsity Christian Fellowship, International Justice Mission, the Accord Network, Eastern University, Multnomah University, George Fox University, Messiah College, Houghton College, Uganda Christian University, Payap University, and others. May this work help equip those called to bring the Good News to the poor as vessels that are themselves an expression of the Gospel.

I am also indebted to our GO ED. advisory board members. Geraldine Sng and George Heng contributed to the first incarnation of this work as a published field guide in journal format. Donna Backues created the water color illustrations of the Mekong, Nile, and Jordan rivers, whose significance will be immediately evident to our GO ED. community and which serve our journey metaphor beautifully. I also acknowledge the generous voluntary assistance of Wilfred Chew in design and layout. I offer special thanks as well to my wife and ministry partner, Adele, who through countless hours of holistic engagement with this subject and its communication, has sustained both this project and its author.

It remains to thank the Lord Jesus Christ, who by owning our poverty delivered us into the riches of his grace.

Solum Deo Gloria

TABLE OF CONTENTS

INTRODUCTION

Despite the fact that our Lord's call is clear to join him in bringing the good news of the Kingdom to the poor, the work of helping people to actually understand poverty remains an important but neglected factor of preparation for service among the vulnerable. The track record of organizations mobilizing people who are not called by God, not equipped, and not themselves participating in transformation, speaks for itself.

Is it any wonder that those working in service among the poor often end up pursuing other goals than those of the Kingdom? We are ill equipped to resist the reductionism and pragmatism that dominate today's development industry. We occupy ourselves in endless self-reporting, attempting to prove to others (donors) and to ourselves our success in "doing good." We find it impossible to shed the values of an entitled, consumerist, competitive global culture and instead end up enacting what is antithetical to our stated Christian beliefs, not to mention infecting others with the same ethos. We have not gained in our education (and cannot seem to find elsewhere) other lenses to discern reality than those given by the dominant materialistic or dualist worldviews of the day. We consequently take and employ the given definitions, no questions asked. This is certainly true of our operational definition of poverty.

We see ourselves as sufficient, and the poor as both needy, alien, and threatening. Our choices and habits in response to this belief reveal an agenda that idolizes power and money, and which sees infrastructure and programs as the solutions to poverty. Consequently, our posture of "service" often comes to resemble that of cultural colonialism. All these things spring from the root of false notions of poverty. This is why the restoration of a biblical theology of poverty is paramount for redeeming everything our ideas about poverty touch, and that is a lot. It is difficult to think of some area that is not effected by what we think about poverty.

Owning Poverty

Our approach to changing our false perceptions and relationships with poverty is summed up in the two words, owning poverty. There is a lot of meaning packed into that juxtaposition. There is of course some irony intended in the concept. Why in the world would anyone want to own poverty? And how can one own something like poverty anyway, which is a lack, a privation? The concept of owning poverty tries to surface the underlying truth that, contrary to the myth of acquisition, our poverty is in fact one of the few things we can truly "own." We shouldn't have too much difficulty with the concept of fiscal responsibility for a net negative, however. We have perfected the life of debt accrual and debt "ownership." If that parallel helps, then owning poverty can be described as taking responsibility for the corporate debt of poverty. The whole world and its socio-economic system is indeed responsible for generating this debt of poverty, like some huge pile of waste that we all created together, but which we have concentrated and located in certain "low value" areas just out of sight. We prefer to enjoy the benefits of that same system undisturbed by the smells of our waste by-product. It may be out of town, but poverty is very much *our* landfill, belonging to us all. Owning means stewarding all that we have generated, not just the good intentions or the beautiful benefits. In addition, owning poverty carries the sense of "owning up to" (admitting) poverty. Because of our contributions to impoverishing others (including reinforcing unjust structures which serve to bolster our privilege), we often deny both our own and others' poverty.

Poverty is a shared human condition. However, much of contemporary life is a delusional attempt to build individual wealth and power as a buffer to calamity and a veil to hide from the fact of our interdependence and vulnerability. If indeed we are all poor and share the fundamental poverty of the human condition, we should learn to own that rather than live in the denial that generates so much of the very avoidance, exclusion and oppression of the materially poor, who we fear will reveal us for what we are...poor like them. Owning poverty argues for identifying with the poor, rather than artificially separating ourselves from them. This relationship of identity with poverty leads to greater authenticity in our relationship with God and deeper solidarity in our relationships with others. As I grow aware of my own poverties (and they are many), no room is left for superiority or self-righteousness, I can only authentically approach the other as one poor person to another.

Transformational Knowledge

This book takes a formational approach to the process of learning about poverty, which starts from the premise that our transformation by God is both the proper means and end of this knowledge. How we know (our epistemology) informs the qualitatively different kinds of knowledge we gain. The mode of enquiry must match what is known. For example, people created *Imago Dei* (in the image of God), with all the irreducible dignities and freedoms that confers, must not be known as (or treated like) unconscious, inanimate things, objects to be reduced and controlled in order to be "known". Attempt to "know" a person as if they were an object, and you will quickly learn the limits of science.[1]

---

[1] On culture and diverse epistemologies see Hiebert, Paul *Transforming Worldviews: an Anthropological Understanding of How People Change* (Grand Rapids: Baker Academic, 2008).

In *Owning Poverty*, we want to intentionally seek to know poverty in a very different, theological and transformational mode. To speak about knowing something theologically is to introduce important concepts including, most obviously, that this epistemology somehow involves God. It is very clear that seeking to know God (or his world through him), is not the same as putting God under a microscope. He is the ultimate Other and Subject, and as such requires us to submit in awe to his larger truths. We are not the big thing, manipulating tiny objects, controlling the variables and judging all things by and for ourselves. We are the small things, encountering a truth that picks us up and does with us whatever it wants. What we know of God and his world are on his terms. Augustine articulated this by describing God as both the Light which we seek and the Light by which we see him.[2] This means that by self-revelation, God himself is intimately and actively involved in our knowledge of poverty.

Owning Poverty invites us to pursue an understanding of poverty with necessary reference to God, with the kind of knowledge that is only to be found in and through God, but also with our whole persons engaged in an epistemology of faith, hope, and love. Such an authentic encounter between poverty "out there" and "in here", promises to not merely change our minds but transform our very capacities to know and to be known, to become fruits of Christ's redemption, the pattern of owning poverty.

Orientation to the Structure

Since this study is designed to facilitate a spiritual journey, the world of travel will provide useful language to speak about what we are experiencing. Your spiritual journey is not to be confused with physical motion across geographical space (although moving our feet in pilgrimage is a well-recognized potential aid to spiritual "motion" in the right direction). We'll use the journey as a metaphor (and we are far from the first to do so) to speak of spiritual transformation. We intend to stop well short of allegorizing, and we needn't refer to each other as "Pilgrim Joe" or anything like that. Journey is a literary device, and to the extent that it helps us organize a complex subject matter or reminds us of the important *steps in a process* (can't escape the metaphor), it is welcome.

In addition to the reading and journaling facilitated by this book, there are several processes that provide a structure for this journey. The structure seeks to facilitate the traveller's engagement with others. The object of a journey is not to wander around alone and lost, but to ask directions from reliable sources.

---

[2] Augustine of Hippo. *On the Holy Trinity* in *Nicene and Post-nicene Fathers First Series, Vol III St. Augustine* Ed. Philip Schaff (New York: Cosimo Classics, 2007) Book VII, p. 108.

"Taking a Bearing" Sections
The map metaphor of Taking a Bearing speaks of capturing a reading of right where you are spiritually in relation to everything else around you. Sometimes this means discovering you were not where you thought you were, or not heading where you thought you were heading. You had better know where you are and what kind of terrain you have to get through and impediments you have to surmount to get there. This section is designed to provide the theological lay of the land, to speak truthfully about things where they lie. The strange objects in this landscape are beliefs and ideas, cultures and values, as well as environmental factors and actions.

"Charting a Course" Sections
To continue with the analogy, the Word of God provides the compass to reorient ourselves to the truth. Scripture is the ultimate corrective for our wayward tendencies, our lostness. It makes sense that after we take a bearing of where we are, we then chart a course to where God wants us to be. Journeys are by definition moving from here to there, from point A to point B. So how do I get from point A to point B in my beliefs, attitudes and actions? His way is clear. "He has shown thee, Oh man what is good and what the Lord requires of you..." (Micah 6:8). If I have drifted, if my life is off course or at a crossroads, I must return to God's word.

"Ancient Roadmaps" Sections
In addition to the word of God, we note in this section the work of those who long ago marked out their routes as they progressed the same journey to know poverty. The whole of Christian tradition in this matter is a guide neglected to our peril. The entire route ancient travelers used may not still be passable today, but they nonetheless give us instruction in pioneering suitable passageways through rough terrain. As you seek a way, it will help to know where you are crossing paths of others who sought the same knowledge you do. Their roads are often the work of a lifetime or even generations, whereas we so often seek shortcuts and make shoddy paths for those who follow. This section will provide road markers and give travelers directions for further cartographic study of these ancient routes. One unique aspect of the Ancient Roadmaps approach is our use of the traditional Christian disciplines as epistemology. The spiritual disciplines of privation are especially important experiential and liturgical modes, which we have been given as a way to understand different aspects of poverty beyond merely "thinking about" them. The traditional Christian spiritual disciplines provide a radically different kind of knowledge from theoretical study. This section seeks to give some context to the disciplines as valid responses to poverty and to provide an important corrective on purely analytical approaches.

We cannot know poverty fully by merely engaging our heads to read about it. Of course, this only works, if those engaged in this journey actually *practice* rather than merely study the disciplines in the Ancient Roadmaps. The practice of the disciplines in the right spirit will teach and shape you in ways thinking alone cannot. Ancient Roadmaps also seeks to present the mode of the disciplines as normative for all those following Christ and still very useful to God as a catalyst for our change. It is hoped that some will choose to explore and walk those tried and tested ways of poverty beyond the introduction offered in this book.

Questions
At the end of each chapter this book provides a set of questions. The questions are meant to facilitate engagement with three different audiences. The first important voice we want you to hear on the journey is that of your **guides**. Those who lead you in this study on poverty, perhaps those who are already in the field of international Christian work or transformational development, might be your guides. Their status is not that of ancient map maker, but they have taken a bearing before. In fact, they are likely to be just up ahead on the same road, and the pitfalls and milestones are fresh in their memory. Ask them what they've seen and experienced. Ask them why they think things are the way they are. Ask them how long they've been that way, how they got that way, and how they might change.

Another kind of intentional engagement is with your **companions**, your peers and fellow travelers. Through discussion and dialogue in a group you are able to benefit from what someone else is seeing at the same time from their perspective. Sometimes their vantage point is just what you needed to understand. We should be walking with others on this journey, and you will find yourself falling into stride with different people at different times. Take the opportunity to hear and share with them, and above all, to enjoy their companionship along the way.

The third kind of dialogue we want this book to facilitate is the one in your **journal**. Journaling is the regular record that enables you to process and deepen experiences through reflection. The name journal suggests that you should write in it daily (*diurnalis* reveals the Latin root, similar to *diarium,* the root of diary, or *buon giorno*, Italian for 'good day'). However, it is more important that you develop a rhythm and habit than adhere to strict frequency guidelines. Likewise, the style can also vary. You can write observational notes in a scientific style, letters to yourself, psalms to God, star date supplemental logs; any style you want. The literary voice matters less than the authenticity of the voice. Be real, and you will be amazed what a useful tool your honesty will be. First and foremost, a journal is an awareness tool. It captures the experiences, feelings and thoughts of the traveler along the journey. You may find that journaling can also provide an aide to help you in many of your ongoing field projects and work assignments. The journal questions are meant to trigger personal reflection and writing on the themes discussed in each chapter. If you are ever short of further prompts, go back to the basics, asking yourself what you observe, how you interpret what you are experiencing, and what you think/feel/believe about what you've seen.

Every good traveler knows that journaling is half the journey. So readers, your are encouraged to be writers as well, setting aside regular space and time to journal. Feel free to augment your writing with other forms of capturing the moment (sketches, pictures, flower pressings, thumb prints; you get the idea). We hope that you will be journaling regularly during your time in this study. We pray also that your capacity to look both outwardly and inwardly at poverty will grow as a result and be assisted by *Owning Poverty*.

Logistics

Owning Poverty is designed for engagement and reflective dialogue on these issues *in community* and ideally in a cross-cultural context outside of our comfort zone. Now that you have acquainted yourself with the structure of this study and chosen your companions on the journey, we recommend your guides set up regular meeting times. The chapters are best processed in groups of 12 people or less and should be divided into smaller groups for break out sessions when possible. In a pinch, the study can be undertaken with a buddy or even as a private devotion, but that is not ideal. The sessions, especially the spiritual disciplines described in the Ancient Roadmaps, can definitely be practiced alone during field work and other times of solitude and isolation, but walking through this study in community will be important, even if you end up exploring many aspects apart from the group. Take advantage of the times you can meet and discuss together (even virtually). We pray you will be challenged and confirmed by God's word and by the testimony of Christians across history who have thought, wrestled and prayed about poverty. It will serve its purpose in your life and the lives of those around you to the extent that you open up and share what you are going through in your journey and listen to others. No book can serve as a roadmap for all experiences; it can only trigger questions and craft a context for engagement. It only comes to life as all bring their experiences and engage humbly and authentically with the Spirit of God, with the truth of scripture, and with the body of Christ.

POVERTY & JOURNEY

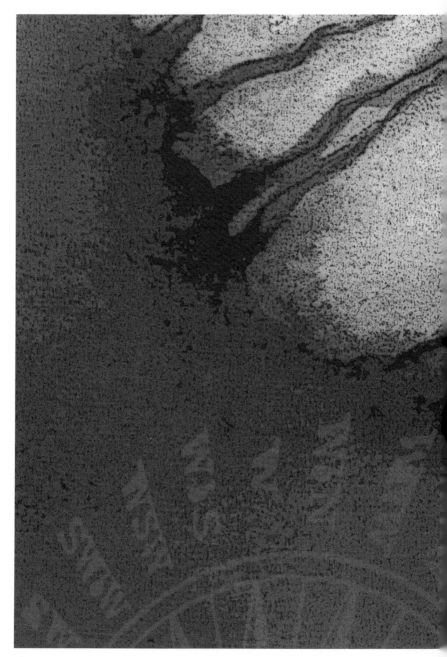

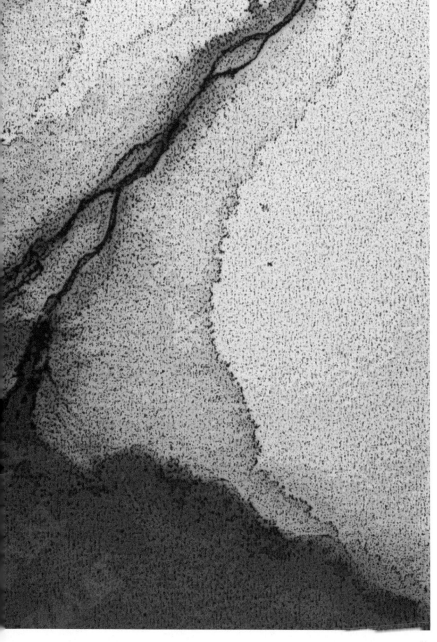

Taking a Bearing

Why and How must I go?

One common response to God's call to go abroad is to question why. Those around us (or our own hearts) argue, "there is plenty for us to experience, learn and do right here. And if you want to help people, there are also plenty of needs right at home." There is some merit in the argument. However, in some very fundamental ways, we can say that it is not "just as effective" to stay...if the goal is transformation.

For one, cross-cultural engagement is a unique factor in spiritual transformation for others and us. A new context often enables us to see poverties that are present at home and in ourselves but previously invisible. We simply lack the capacity to see what is familiar, and we desperately need to go in order to allow the change in scenery to remedy that peculiar brand of familiarity blindness. We also know that *the way* we see things has been deeply shaped by our worldview. Until we go outside of our own culture, we don't even recognize that we have a worldview, let alone have the discernment to tease apart what is true, beautiful, and good in our own culture from what is false, marred, and life destroying. A fish never thinks about water until it is out of it.

Thirdly, one's own culture tends to provide a certain comfort that can create inertia against needed change. We like sameness; we do not want to think too hard about things. In the comfort zone of our own culture, we can just cruise through life on autopilot. Consequently, we often take the cultural forms of life off the shelf, employing them without question. If God wants to call us to employ ways or forms of life that are different from the world, in order to signpost something important in his Kingdom, we can give him a broader palette to work with by going abroad. To go and experience how other people do life and relationships and live out their Christian faith in very different contexts is to gain wisdom about how to incarnate our own faith intentionally.

If, however, the only reasons we go abroad are for a tourist experience or because we are fulfilling an imagined role as savior, we are impeding transformation. It isn't geography that is the key here, but rather posture. It is not *where*, but *how* we go that matters. The first thing that needs to be changed in our posture is to shed modern notions of what it means to travel. The modern tourist seeks sights and experiences, often eclectic and of variable interest to them. That is essentially applying a consumer posture to places and cultures and seeing travel as an end in itself, with the tourist as the ultimate judge of the value of the experiences (which are also ranked for other tourists in TripAdvisor). The tourist's transactional relationship with the host culture minimizes its potential transformational impact on the visitor (because the one with the money governs the terms and distance of the relationship). The tourist's photographic record of images on their trip also captures and mediates their experiences as products the foreign culture provides them.

If we add to this the peculiar habits of our "Selfie" generation, it makes a change in travel posture more difficult. We need a noun to describe this new quality that shapes so much of contemporary life; let's call it "Selfieness." Selfieness is in one sense a feeling or belief that a personal experience is only valid or legitimate if it was digitally captured and posted online. Until it is on some social network for all to see, it didn't happen. Selfieness is more importantly the compulsion to frame one's self within that valid record of experience. Most dangerous of all is the temptation to record a picture of ourselves "doing good." At one level, selfieness reveals a genuine craving to integrate, to be a part of the world. However, it also highlights a displacement of healthy reciprocal feedback of traditional human engagement, with superficial evidence that "we were there." It reinforces a narcissistic lens on culture. If we are not careful we may find ourselves spending our energy abroad looking for a unique backdrop to frame ourselves or add texture to our profile. If on the other hand, we can resist selfieness, we may grow the eyes to discern the beauty of cultures and peoples in God's bigger story and a desire to communicate dignity.

The other significant posture change required, especially for travel to developing contexts, is shedding the savior complex. There are some who are driven to go by a need to be needed. People from the global north can often act as if they are the sole source of help. If we start from a false sense of self-superiority or superiority of culture, we will measure 'them' by what they lack compared to 'us' and 'ours'. We will also continue to be frustrated (and frustrate others) by our impulse to fix them. Why can't they do this? What is wrong with them? If we go looking only for what is wrong, we will find it. But we are told to dwell on whatsoever things are pure, lovely and of good repute (Phil 4:8). That is a healthy posture in any context, but especially when encountering other cultures.

As we go abroad, we have to ask ourselves if we are traveling to consume, going merely to seek one more experience to entertain us or to adorn our profile? Or are we willing to allow God to put us into a bigger frame and story, where the self is not at the center of the camera's focus? Are we willing to let the cross-cultural encounter judge and change us, instead of vice versa? Can we go primarily to learn and listen rather than to tell and teach, and go to be changed, rather than to fix? Instead of poverty tourism, can we go seeking mutual transformation?

Charting a Course
Read Luke 10:1-37, Matt 28:16-20

The Greeks had a word *splagchnizomai* (which sounds like a sneeze). It means to be moved in your internal guts. We translate it as being moved with compassion, and it points to a reality of human experience, namely, that some truths are best appropriated by ingestion. Jesus Christ was frequently moved with compassion. He did not visit our world as a tourist, but brought humanity and all its hurts into himself and felt them deeply in his guts. His incarnation (our means of salvation and model of ministry) went both ways. He came down into the midst of us; he also took us all inside of himself. There is a big difference in merely being somewhere, even seeing something first-hand, and taking it in. Until poverty is taken into our selves and allowed to upset our stomach, it is not really a truth that we can be said to "own", even though we might acknowledge it as an undisputed fact or remember the statistics involved in this or that injustice. Psychology calls this internalization, which echoes the important distinction between a world of information *out there*, and things we allow to shape us *in here*.

There is this repeating pattern of going, internalization, compassion, and action in the way Christ travelled. Everywhere he went, he met people where they were at. Everywhere he met them in their various poverties, he was moved with compassion. Every time he was moved with compassion, he engaged more deeply into the lives of the people he had encountered. He saw the crowds were like sheep without a shepherd, and he was moved with compassion and began teaching them (Matt 9:36, Mark 6:34). He was moved with compassion and healed their sick (Matt 14:14). He was moved with compassion and fed them (Matt 15:32, Mark 8:2). He was moved with compassion and gave sight to the blind (Matt 20:34). He was moved with compassion and cleansed a leper and restored him to community (Mark 1:41). He was moved with compassion and freed a demoniac from possession (Mark 9:22). He was moved with compassion and raised a woman's son from the dead (Luke 7:13). Even in his parables, his lead characters were moved with compassion to action. The neighborly Samaritan was moved with compassion and nursed and cared for the man beaten and robbed (Luke 10:33). The master was moved with compassion and forgave the debt of his slave (Matt 18:27). The father of the prodigal son was moved with compassion when he saw his son coming down the road, and he fell on his neck and kissed him. He restored his clothes and his place of honor in the family (Luke 15:20).

Think about the opposite picture. If we see someone who lacks compassion or refuses to be moved to compassion, it usually reveals that they see themselves as above the other person. They see the conditions of the other's poverties as chiefly the poor's own fault, and they blame the other person for not being as hard working or resourceful, essentially for not being as good as they are. They are not moved with compassion because they do not take the other inside; they do not bring the other into their guts because they believe the other is unworthy of compassion. The implicit judgment is that they themselves are worthy of what they have received, but the other's case lacks merit. The other does not deserve mercy. We are told to do justly, love mercy, and to walk humbly with our God (Micah 6:8). This is not a common posture. Far more common is disdain, disgust, distance. This is because we are much more likely to explain others' negative behavior or conditions in terms of bad character or blame it on their personality, while ignoring the surrounding situational factors. Whereas we are far more likely to attribute our own less than perfect behavior and conditions to external causes and extenuating circumstances.[1]

Hebrews 5:2 explains, "He can have compassion on those who are ignorant and going astray, since he himself is also subject to weakness." This means that Christ's capacity to be moved by both our condition and our circumstances is proportional to how low he was prepared to go to meet us (Phil 2:5). He was prepared to subject himself to a station as low as us. This says a lot about the way we are to go. As with Christ, it is our weakness that makes us best suited to encountering the other in the same way Christ did, with compassion. Unlike Christ, we are not climbing down from Heaven to meet humanity in low estate. We are not infinitely above the human station but share its poverty and shame. Compassion should move us more readily because our own poverties are so much more readily apparent.

This picture of compassion spells out the terrain of this journey, for if poverty is allowed to engage us inside, our experience will be characterized by things of the interior life, our thoughts and emotions and the (sometimes unfamiliar) movements of our spirit. Many of you will identify with being moved inside with compassion even to initiate this journey in the first place. No doubt, you will continue to strongly feel stuff in your gut throughout the journey that craves explanation, analysis, consolation. Sometimes the only consolation on offer will be a resonance with others who feel and have felt things similar to you and an impetus to engage more deeply in obedient acts of love.

---

[1] Heider, F. *The Psychology of Interpersonal Relations* (New York: Wiley, 1958). Larson, J.R. "Evidence for a self-serving bias in the attribution of causality" *Journal of Personality* (1977) 45(3), 430-441.

Our heart sets our feet in motion, but sometimes it works the other way around. Physically moving ourselves in pilgrimage to pursue the sacred in a place can draw our spirit into pursuit of God.

The Discipline of Pilgrimage

"Come and see", "Follow me", "I go to prepare a place for you" "As the Father sent me, so send I you", "Go ye into all the world"; if you haven't noticed, our faith always seems to be in motion. Long before we were (pejoratively) called "Christians" we were known as "The Way", which is also something Jesus called himself. It is strange that Christ should call himself a road and then call us to go on that road (John 14:6). No one is told, "no, don't get up; you're fine; you can stay put; no need to go far."

Jesus Christ himself always seemed to be journeying somewhere. He must have walked thousands of miles in the years of his earthly life and ministry, all around Galilee, Samaria, Judea, and in and around Jerusalem. Once someone promised to follow him anywhere, he responded, "Foxes have holes and birds of the air have nests, but the Son of Man has nowhere to lay his head" (Matt 8:20). This is as much to say that Christ's way was not toward the comforts of home, toward the settled life, but a journey into and beyond suffering. The Gospel of Luke in particular emphasizes the travel narrative of Jesus "setting his face toward Jerusalem" (Luke 9:51) and reinforcing some 17 times that throughout his ministry, Jesus was always "on his way." In this Jesus provides continuity in a long line of biblical images of journey, from Abraham's wanderings toward the promised land, and the exodus of Israel out of Egypt, to the itinerant prophets. His own journey narrative he describes as "coming down from heaven" "to do the will of him who sent me". He took the *via dolorosa*, the way of suffering to the cross and death, descended to the dead, rose and ascended "returning to the Father." If his destination were just a physical place, Christ would have been content to have arrived in procession in Jerusalem to Hosannas and to restore the land of Israel at that time. Instead, he gained the world as his Kingdom and his territory, thereby setting in motion the redemption of the whole earth. In this, Christ modeled for all his disciples this way of sojourning through the world, seeking the Kingdom of God, our home in him, rather than in some other land. He then sent us out to be pilgrims in the same way (Luke 10).

The written record of Christian pilgrimage is present as early as the fourth century, and the tradition of those seeking to visit the sacred places particularly those associated with the life and miracles of Jesus Christ and his apostles is much older. "Places and buildings do carry memory, power and hope, ...places where Jesus walked and talked, suffered, died and rose again, can and do resonate with the meaning of what he did."[2] However, pilgrimage is not merely sight seeing, nor traveling to special places in order to find answers to our questions. Instead, it is giving God permission to use those places to give us new questions. Since pilgrimage is simultaneously motion in the spiritual plane and the physical plane, the most important things one can pack for the journey is the expectation to encounter God in both.

Expect God to be present everywhere.
God is present everywhere in his world. The whole earth is the holy land. All places have sacred significance, and all people bear the image of God. No part of creation escapes his notice and his Presence.

Expect God to reveal himself anywhere.
God from the creation of his world has been engaged with it. He walked in the garden in the cool of the morning with Adam and Eve. He is incessantly involved in the affairs of human history. God, ever-present can be revealed at any moment, around any corner, in any encounter.

Expect God to reveal his Presence in sacred places.
Although no place where his Spirit is, has more or less of him, there are certain places that have become signs of the presence of the Creator because they are sites of unique redemptive acts of God in human history. We are called to worship him in Spirit and in truth everywhere (John 4:23). In some places that call just seems to be louder.

Expect God to be uniquely present in sacred places of suffering.
Because God's heart is near to those who are of a broken and contrite heart, we can expect the Christ who suffered on the cross to continue to be where humanity suffers. There are several sacred places of suffering, which we should consider holy ground. These wounds on the earth, for example places of genocide and exploitation, remind us more vividly of our human poverty, our capacity for evil, our need for God. You must go and discern in those places that seem God-forsaken, that God was and is indeed right there in the suffering of his world.

Expect God to meet you where he leads you.
God will be where he is calling you. He is already here in a special way. He is present and has been working here in this place for a long time. It may be a new place to you, but it is not new to him. Discern the special ways God's care and presence and glory are here. He may choose to reveal himself differently to you in this new place.

---

[2] Wright, N.T. *The Way of the Lord: Christian Pilgrimage Today* (Cambridge: Erdmans, 2014).

Practice: As you leave your place of familiarity and home and begin your journey, ask God to give you the heart of a pilgrim, expecting the presence of God everywhere and being present yourself. Ask him to speak to you specifically through your encounter with this place, to use your physical and cultural dislocation, your wanderings and searchings, to prompt real motion of your heart in pursuit of him. Then ask him to guide you and to reveal himself to you, to meet you in this place in a unique way of his choosing. Ask him to lead you and to come and find you.

Questions: Poverty & Journey

Guides

Introduce yourself
Once you have been assigned your group, let them know a bit about your background and what about the subject matter poverty motivates and interests you.

Past experiences
What are your past experiences of devotional approaches? Give some examples from your experiences to the group of small group Bible studies that worked well and explain why they worked.

Companions

Hopes for the Journey
This study is grounded in the objective: to transform the next generation to own and end poverty. Our hope to have a transforming encounter with God is accompanied by hundreds of other hopes we have for what we might discover on this journey, what relationships we might build along the way, and what fruit this journey might bear in our lives. Take some time now to share our hopes for this study with the group.

Journal

Starting Good Habits
How should I speak and whom should I address in my journal?

How in the world did I get here? What were the events, people and thoughts in my life that conspired to bring me here to this new place?

What are my first impressions of this place?

POVERTY & PERCEPTION

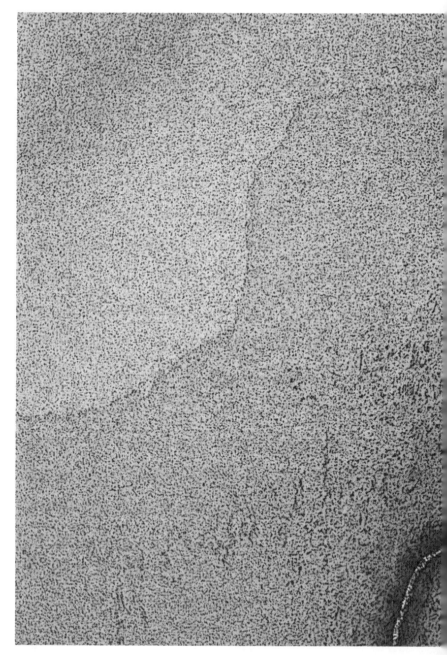

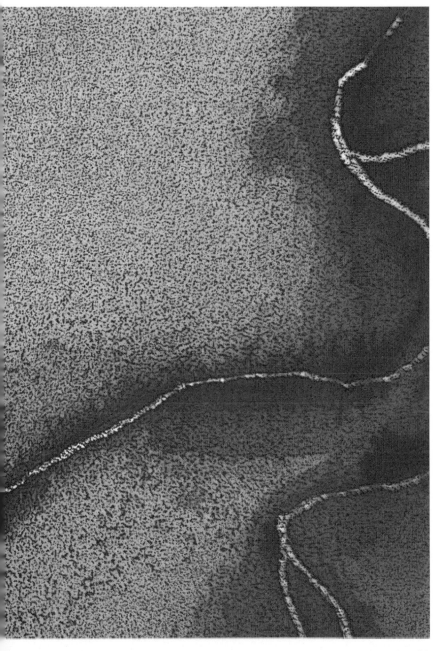

Taking a Bearing
Poverty takes many shapes.

When someone asks us to describe what physical poverty looks like, we have little difficulty coming up with images. We see bodies of emaciated children, homeless people in cardboard boxes, shanty towns, slums. Perhaps your mind goes to Stan Grossfeld's Pulitzer prize winning image of a gaunt-eyed Ethiopian woman wrapped around her child like a shroud.[1] Both are in the obvious final throes of starvation, but something in the composition does not allow us to look away nor distance ourselves from them as objects of disdain. Her covered head evokes the Christian archetypal imagery of Madonna and child. Her hands on her child's head seem to say, "behold my son is also the holy *Imago Dei* (image of God)."

It was an image that struck a chord in the 1980s, created awareness in an American context plunging headlong into a "me" culture, Reaganomics, and living the Wall Street mantra "greed is good." The image provided an essential crack in the facade that Western values were essentially, intrinsically good. As effective as this kind of imagery is in raising awareness, it also has the effect of training our eye toward a certain type of poverty to the neglect of other equally dehumanizing (but less visible) forms of poverty. For example, what do we think of when we speak of other kinds of poverty (spiritual, social, mental, cultural, moral, etc.)? The images are not so clear or ready to mind.

It is a physiological fact that the human eye has a natural blind spot at the center of our retina. We notice it when we try to look directly at objects that are far away. Astronomers advise looking peripherally to avoid this blind spot when identifying the faint, distant lights of heavenly bodies. There is a parallel experience when looking at poverty. Not only is it difficult to bring into focus and to define, it seems to evade us the more directly we look at it. This not only suggests that there is something wrong with our overly simplistic definitions of this inherently complex object in our field of vision. But some of the most insidious forms of poverty hide from the light, evade public view (like exploitation in the sex trade). However, poverty blindness also suggests a limitation in the instrumentation. Sometimes there is a glaring poverty right in front of us. We have serious blind spots.

Sometimes perception of poverty can be achieved by indirect vision. If we look at our interior landscape of poverty we may learn something of poverty in the exterior, out of the corner of our eye, as it were. Or

---

[1] http://www.pulitzer.org/awards/1985

conversely, we may learn something of the spiritual aspects of poverty by looking at the physical. Another kind of indirect perception is to look at the multifaceted features of the experience of poverty in order to build up a composite outline of its nature from its effects. In this way, we understand what poverty is by understanding what it is like for those experiencing it.

The experience of poverty can mean inequality, disparity, vulnerability, physical limitation, ethnic & gender discrimination, social exclusion, disempowerment by institutions, exploitation, victimization, hunger, inability to make commitments, lack of access to basic needs (water, food, shelter, health care), compounding debt, lack of opportunity, voicelessness, fear, absence of generosity, powerlessness, slavery, addiction, violence, lack of knowledge, injustice, hopelessness, loss of emotional resilience, absence of community, generational degradation. Poverty can manifest itself in many ways that might not match our image or not appear at all in our blind spots. We require a transformation of capacity in us, the instruments, in order to perceive and own poverty.

This study is seeking to facilitate a personal engagement with a reality that promises to have a profound impact on our Christian faith and walk. The context you find yourself in now should begin to unravel the myth that poverty can be understood as a mere abstract concept for intellectual study. You are already beginning to experience and perceive it in different ways. What we hope this study becomes is a tool for interpreting your experience and a catalyst for further transformation.

Charting a Course
Read 2 Corinthians 8.
Even though we remember something vaguely about God's grace being made perfect in weakness, we wonder if focusing on poverty isn't a bit of a downer, creating a bunch of depressed people, by thinking about what we and others lack. Shouldn't we rather just focus on the positive, work to our strengths rather than weaknesses? There are at least two things wrong with the strengths approach. First, pretending poverty doesn't exist doesn't make it go away, and second, the generosity that alleviates the very real poverty in the world does not grow by focusing on building up more of what we have. When people speak of giving, it is often contingent. "If I get this, I will give. If you do this for me, God, I will make this great sacrificial gift." Or "If I were a millionaire, I would be able to do so much good, so I will focus on building my business or ministry until I achieve that (retreating) point of wealth." This pretends that after years of focusing on damming the river, suddenly one day when the water level is high enough, we will open up the flood gates. It is more likely that we will just build a hydroelectric facility to benefit ourselves more and pretend

that we are generous for what we let trickle downstream. Even more delusional, is when someone loses a lot of money on the stock market and they declare, "If I would have known I was going to lose it, I would have given it away." We try to control the future by our wealth. We are paralyzed from giving by the need to create a buffer against our own calamity. We are taught to operate like those folk who store up canned goods in a bomb shelter in their back yard in preparation for the coming Apocalypse, not noticing that for those already suffering poverty today, it is "Apocalypse Now."

None of our typical notions of rich philanthropists giving to poor people have much to do with real generosity. One of the first things we notice about real generosity is that it seems to work out of all sense of proportion. People surprise us in their giving out of apparent poverty. Paul aptly describes the Macedonian churches' donation as "the abundance of their joy in much tribulation and their deep poverty abounding to the riches of their liberality." Real generosity flows from a combination of two essential ingredients. One is an identification with those in poverty, and the other is a faith in the gift-giving nature of God. Both of these things come from experience. If one believes themselves the mere recipients of the generosity of God, they are anything but downers. They overflow. Those who know the meaning of their lack (and the gift that alleviated it) are the ones who say "help yourself; I've got so much; it's not like it's really mine, and there's more where that came from." But it is those who operate by fear because they have never admitted their poverty (and consequently never experienced the generosity of God by receiving) who say, "Hey, that's mine; I only have so much; I earned it, and I don't owe nobody nothin'!" It is also obvious that those who see their wealth as earned create a distinction, separating themselves from the poor. Whereas the embrace of the poor by those who see they are also poor is not strange. Verse 9 sets the framework for an entire Christian worldview of generosity. You know (you have experienced) the grace of our Lord Jesus Christ (the favor of the unearned gift of being embraced into the household of God), that being rich (having all resources and being the only source of all goodness), for your sakes he became poor (for mankind subjecting himself to the ups and downs of human life and substituting himself as the ransom for sin, and taking on our deepest spiritual poverty), that you by his poverty might become rich (his voluntary emptying of himself awarded to us all the riches of God's whole self in Christ).

This motif of describing what Christ did in economic terms repeats itself throughout the New Testament and is not to be taken to mean "follow Christ and you will get money." It is a metaphor to speak of the "riches of

God's grace." People raised in church-going families may be over-familiar with the word, grace, or think of it as a one-time transaction. Grace reveals that all of life is a gift; the world we live in is a gift world. That is the true nature of the cosmos, because it is the nature of the God behind all, the Giver of all good things. He makes his rain to fall on the just and the unjust. Consequently, the Kingdom of God is also a grace economy, a gift economy, a potluck. Christ calls all to receive by faith; no merit is earned or deserved; everything is gift. This also means we are all charity cases, bringing no inherent moral or other good that would improve our standing with God or even our relative standing over others. It may be more blessed to give than to receive, but it is harder to receive. We don't like being needy. Only as we acknowledge our bankruptcy can we receive from God, and only as we receive God's generosity can we channel God's generosity toward others. Paul claims that this equality is what characterizes God's household. In light of the disparity between the rich and poor in our day, this is also a word of freedom from fear of loss.

Paul addresses fear head on when he says, I'm not asking you to give so that others can be rescued and you suffer instead. That is not the outcome of generosity at all. It is equality. Your abundance makes up for their lack, and their abundance makes up for your lack. This equality principle is true both in the sense of different parts of the body at different times or places of abundance and want, but also in terms of different types of poverty and abundance. Right now your community may be rich in one thing but poor in another, while some other community is rich and poor in other ways. We experience equality and generosity as we encounter more of God's body and world as a gift economy.

Ancient Roadmaps
The Christian spiritual disciplines are signs of different aspects of poverty. The chief function of these types of voluntary privation is to remind us of our lack and restore our faith in the abundant provision of God.

The Disciplines of Privation
Poverty points to grace in the Christian Disciplines. The Christian disciplines of poverty are explicitly not about asceticism, nor some sense of merit earned from depriving one's self. It is also not a means of defeating evil by hurting the body. The body in the Christian faith is affirmed as integral to the whole person (called the soul) which God created and redeemed, and which he doubly affirmed by his incarnation and resurrection. Furthermore, the transformation of the will, the source of human sin, the root of the problem, is not effected by works, but by the Spirit of God as a gracious gift through Christ Jesus. So what do the disciplines of privation (acts of willingly giving up something) signify, and

why pursue them? It seems strange to be given something by taking something away rather than adding, but that is the nature of knowledge through the spiritual disciplines. If we look at some obvious disciplines of privation (taking away) we begin to notice their relationship to poverty:

fasting (voluntary privation of food)
simplicity (voluntary privation of busyness)
renunciation (voluntary privation of possessions)
watching (voluntary privation of sleep)
silence (voluntary privation of speech)
solitude (voluntary privation of human company)
submission (voluntary privation of free will in obedience)

Each of these disciplines corresponds to an aspect of the experience of human poverty (the lack of resources, hunger, restlessness, anxiety, voicelessness, alienation, exclusion, powerlessness, etc.). In their correspondence with an aspect of the shared human condition of poverty, each discipline becomes an act of identification with that truth and also a Christ-imitating act of solidarity with others in their suffering. True practice of the spiritual disciplines does just the opposite of separating us by merit; it draws us all down closer to the true ground of our equality. This helps us understand the biblical notion that the disciplines were instituted not to afflict one's self but as a catalyst to liberate others from injustice (Isaiah 58:5-8), which is only possible in the shared equality of poverty.

When we further consider other disciplines like confession (voluntary admission of our moral depravity and our poverty of love for God and others) or prayer (voluntary petition and supplication of God in the posture of a beggar) we realize that this theme of poverty, this posture of poverty is normative. It is not supposed to leave us after we become Christians. The same grace by which we were received continues to be operative in God's household every day. This same posture of poverty also ultimately finds its fruition in other Christian disciplines that flow from the gifts of God to us in our poverty, the disciplines of worship, thanksgiving, and generosity.[2]

Practice: *Identify at least one discipline of privation that you have never practiced, and discuss it with God in prayer. In particular ask him to create a desire to have him reveal some aspect of poverty (your own and others') through your participation in one or more of the disciplines.*

---

[2] The spiritual formation approach is deeply indebted to Foster, Richard J. *Celebration of Discipline: the Path to Spiritual Growth* (San Francisco: Harper & Row, 1978). Leech, Kenneth. *True Prayer: An Invitation to Christian Spirituality* (Morehouse,1995). Willard, *Dallas Spirit of the Disciplines: Understanding How God Changes Lives* (HarperCollins,1988).

Questions: Poverty & Perception

Guides
Definitions
How has seeing different kinds of poverty effected your worldview (especially your definition of poverty and wealth)?

Companions
Visible & Invisible
What kinds of poverty are more visible/less visible to us?

Do our different cultures have different blind spots to our own types of poverty?

What are some ways we can think of to perceive poverty by looking peripherally instead of directly?

Journal
Grace
How does grace equalize everyone as receivers?

Do I give myself permission to lack and to receive?

Potluck
Do I believe and operate as if the world is a meritocracy or a gift/potluck economy?

POVERTY & AUTHORITY

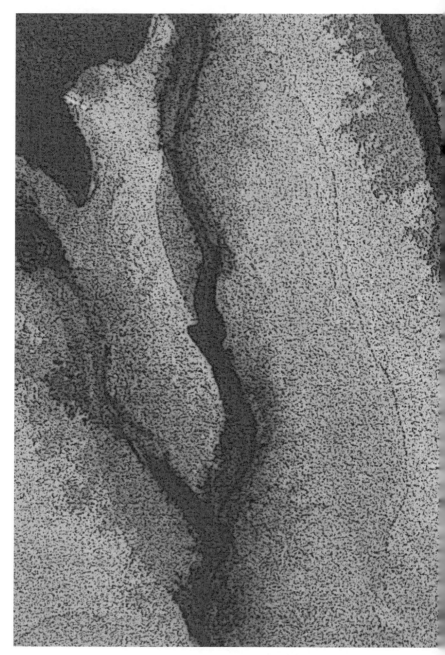

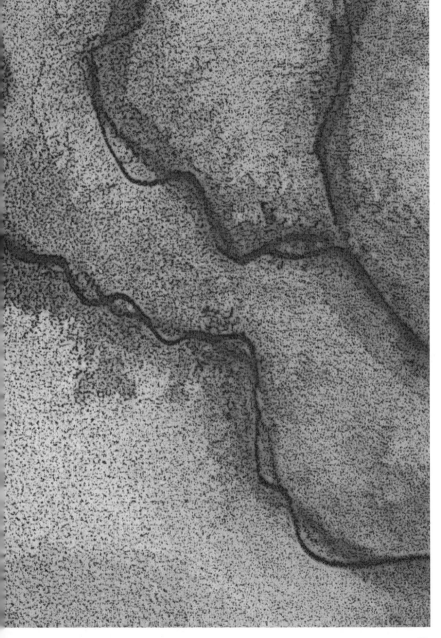

Taking a Bearing
So What? Says Who?

Not everyone shares the same assumptions about the station and role that the Bible is to occupy in our worldview. Wait a minute. Doesn't the question "So what?" obviously lead Christians to the authority of God's word? The answer to why we should care is inextricably linked to the same authority that answers, "Says Who?" The only reason the Bible is authoritative is because it is God who "says so". The authority of God's word should obviously have sway among Christians, who keep calling Jesus, "Lord." But a simple appeal to "the Bible tells me so" is of limited value when Christians, imbibing our culture's relative approach, award minimal authority to God and his word in their lives.

Authorities are what we appeal to as the grounds of our beliefs, where we go for definitive answers for life, especially when there are conflicting views. We have many authorities that exercise a strong influence over our beliefs and our lives. Personal authorities like our family, friends, community, as well as cultural authorities like science, teachers, mass advertising, pop culture, and social media, are constantly correcting and shaping us for good or ill. In a democratic society authority is exercised by influence more than force, by giving us affirmation when we reinforce the values and norms of the world, and by pressuring us to conform by the fear of exclusion or losing out when we do not. However, what is exalted as the chief authority in most of our lives, most of the time, is the self. Even with relation to other authorities, we are advised to withhold absolute submission to any authority but the self and thereby reserve the right to interpret and adjudicate on all things ourselves. We believe it is an infringement of our self autonomy to be corrected by any authority.

What is even more disturbing is the tendency to operate by this extreme authority of individualism in our faith by picking and choosing what we like or what makes us look right, and dumping what we don't like the sound of. When we are in charge of regulating what and when we hear from God, resenting anything from him that seems too much like a command or that thwarts our sensibilities, it is we who are exercising divine authority, not God. The practice of using the scripture to build one's own case or to justify one's own preferences is so common and normal ("you believe what you want, and I believe what I want"), most people have forgotten that another posture is even possible. This has dire consequences with regard to the truth of and response to poverty. A former colleague was working on a brochure that he wanted to leave behind with a group of Christian church, business and government leaders in his city to encourage them to engage. He started the brochure with the vision to transform the city one neighborhood at a time, and the mission to get the whole church to engage the whole person with the whole Gospel across the whole city. Then he moved on to statistics. He was searching for the one statistic that would convince and fire up the whole city, X amount of teens trafficked in the sex trade, X amount of homeless, X amount of children going hungry each night, etc. It became obvious after a while that a statistic wasn't the thing. Statistics only motivate people who share belief in a common truth about the travesty the numbers communicate, a common reason behind why the statistics matter. You could stack statistics (or bodies) up to the sky and people will not care, if they do not already connect the facts to an underlying authoritative truth.

C. F. Andrews (a missionary contemporary with Gandhi) said changing the world requires truth so authoritative that it needs no appeal to anything but itself and its own disruptive presence. "An evil custom," he said, "may be apparently ineradicable, but once set up, in glaring contradiction with it, *one incompatible ideal*, and let it work, and the end of that evil custom is certain."[1] The Gospel needn't prove or shout; it brings about a transformation simply by sitting next to (and defiantly contrasting), the normal structures and authorities of the dominant society, the lies that are so antithetical to it. It is biblical truth that answers both the questions, "So what?" and "Why should I care?". It is apparent that many, operating by the dominant Western culture's assumptions, simply don't care if poverty does not effect them. Or they integrate inconvenient statistics into their current authority structures. Their frameworks reinforce pet notions like the concept of the "deserving poor", or the belief that the global economy by which consumers get their stuff cheaply simply requires injustice as an inevitable fact of life. With their authority of self they argue, "better them than me", and on the authority of a misguided economic theory they displace the truth about the value of all people and erode their own care.

If I don't believe something behind the statistics, namely, humanity's equal worth based on their status as people created in the image of God, and our extraordinary status as beloved in the redemptive work of Christ, the fact that they are my neighbor, my brother, of no less value than my self, what will the numbers matter? What if instead, we actually received this one incompatible ideal that affirms, the least one of these deserves the same care as Christ himself, and Christ attributes our treatment or negligence of the valued vulnerable, to him (Matt 25). The One who values them takes it personally when we don't. If what scripture teaches is the case, then every statistic, any fact that is contrary to the just treatment of their persons will move me to compassionate action.

---

[1] Andrews, Charles Freer *The Ghandian Thought* (Delhi: Akashdeep Pub House, 1990), 73.

Charting a Course
Read Matthew 5:17-48.

Although experience helps us internalize and prove (bullet-proof) truth in our own lives, it is not the foundation of truth for Christians. We trust the words of an Old Friend. "You have heard it said...but I say to you."

We live by faith. At the beginning of this spiritual journey (to understand and live out the truth about poverty) it is important that we establish the primacy of the authority of God's word. Those who come from a Christian background and have heard similar words before, will need to struggle to understand what this means beyond just signing a statement of faith for their church, college, or organization. That is not all that is entailed in awarding the Bible authority in our worldview, the lens through which we see and interpret this crazy planet. We are going to have to frequently reference this compass as a guide along the way; so we had better start with understanding what level of trust God's word requires of us.

One Bible passage that reveals and models for us the meaning of awarding authority to the word of God is Matthew 5:17-48. This passage is an important foundational teaching of Christ because it blew apart a thousand religious and cultural assumptions about the nature of human goodness. The culture of his day, as does our own Western church culture, codified holiness in behaviors so that it was within reach...doable. It is the age-old definition of righteousness as a list of do's and don'ts. Christ's teaching directly contradicted their simplification, and just in case anyone failed to see the difference, he kept employing that rhetorical device "you have heard it said by those of old...but I say to you."

He was making a bold claim for the authority of his word, his take on reality, his definitions. As the fulfillment of the law, the Son of God, overrides all we think we know about the way things are with his word. What this dynamic set up then (and sets up for us today) is a choice. There are many voices, some that have been around a long time, telling us this or that. Then there is this One Voice telling us otherwise. We don't like what it has to say. It spells out a different standard of righteousness that looks at both action and the heart. Do we really want to go there? That would make goodness unattainable for those hoping it is only external.

The authority of scripture is not an abstract concept; it is a choice. In this case, do we throw out Christ's definition or accept the reality he expressed, the harsh conclusion that we are incapable in ourselves of true righteousness? Doesn't it make more sense to have a religious system that we can succeed at? If we keep to our old authority on this subject (one backed up by the biased judgment of our own selves), we come out smelling like roses, and feeling downright justified. Embracing Christ's truth on this matter of what and who is good, is one of the hardest belief choices we will ever (repeatedly) make as Christians. For it most clearly sets up a most uncomfortable dynamic of poverty in light of the authority of scripture, "Let God be true and every man a liar." (Rom 3:4).

To accept God's voice is to silence other voices, including our own, as untrustworthy. "Yes, but in the *real world*", we hear, "Christ's teachings are not practical." Isn't this exactly the point? Who we listen to is our authority, defines what the *real world* is, what is illusion, what "works" or not. God is not interested in us listening to his word as yet another voice, one voice among many, which we ourselves ultimately arbitrate, but as the final word to us on the way things really are and will be.

There is a delightful little episode in the life of one of the early desert Fathers of the church, St. Antony (born mid 3rd century AD). Some followers of Christ came to him seeking an authoritative guide for their lives. He replied to the brothers: "You have heard the Scriptures? They will do very well for you." The brothers were not satisfied and replied, "Father, we would also like a word from you." Then Antony told them, "The Gospel says: if someone strikes you on the right cheek, turn the other to him also." They said: "We cannot do that." The old man said to them: "If you cannot offer the other one, at least allow him to strike you on one cheek." "We cannot even do that", they replied. "If you cannot even do that", said he, "do not pay back the evil you have received." And they said: "We cannot do this either." Then the old man said to his disciple: "Prepare a little broth of corn for them, for they are ill. If you cannot do this, and you will not do that, what can I do for you? You are in need of prayer."[2]

I love that the old man's response was to show them how sick they really were to claim to follow Christ but not follow any of his words. Often seekers come hoping to find an easy word that replaces the hard words of Christ, especially regarding how God sees our poverty and his righteousness. We seek a special word, when the word has already been given. The issue is not ignorance of his word but an unwillingness to hear it and submit in obedience to it. Christians spend a lot of effort trying to reinterpret Jesus' words to reinforce their lifestyle and worldview. "The time will come when people will not put up with sound doctrine. Instead, to suit their own desires, they will gather around them a great number of teachers to say what their itching ears want to hear"(2 Tim 4:3). In our day, we can find voices to say anything. We define our posture towards those authorities by what we "like" or "unlike". Regardless, God still speaks true.

---

[2] Leloir, Louis "Lectio Divina and the Desert Fathers" in *Liturgy*, Vol. 23, n. 2, 1989, 3-38.

Ancient Roadmaps

More than a devotional method or exercise, lectio divina is an attitude of personal reception toward and humble submission under God's word.

The Discipline of *Lectio Divina*

As the words suggest, at its root, *lectio divina* was the practice and principle of treating and hearing scripture as Holy, Divine, as God's Word. The best description of the purpose of this kind of engagement with scripture is that of church historian, Armond Veilleux. He writes, "The tradition of what is now called *lectio divina*, that is to say, the desire to allow oneself to be challenged and transformed by the fire of the Word of God... [this] contact with the Word is contact with the fire that burns, disturbs, calls violently to conversion. Contact with Scripture is not ...a method of prayer; it is a mystical encounter. And this encounter often makes them afraid, insofar as they are conscious of its demands."[3]

The assumption is that this text is "alive and powerful and sharper than any two edged sword" and so shouldn't be treated lightly like some other kind of text. The principle of *lectio divina* was later formalized in monastic traditions into a practice which tried to make it more accessible to the common man by emphasizing a few key actions that facilitate a right posture before scripture. They are as follows:

lectio (reading) - Read the passage the first time slowly allowing his Word to speak directly. In silence recall any images or phrases that captured your attention.

meditatio (meditation) - Read the passage the second time focusing on what is being said through those strong phrases and images. Reflect on the meaning of the words and images. Are there any metaphors and stories that help reveal the passage's significance? Discuss briefly.

oratio (prayer) - In silence pour out your heart in conversation with God himself directly about what he means. What is he trying to convey? Engage in dialogue with God (both speaking and listening, asking and waiting) on this Word.

contemplatio (contemplation)-Read the passage a third time, imagining what would be different if you really believed and received his Word. Reflect on what this word requires of you.

---

[3] Veilleux, Armand. "*Lectio Divina* as School of Prayer Among the Fathers of the Desert", translation of a talk given at the Centre Saint-Louis-des-Français, in Rome, November, 1995.

Lectio divina provides an important tension between two extreme tendencies today to either read the word for an experience of the heart without recourse to the mind, which tends toward emotional subjectivity, or to study the word as a purely intellectual exercise without recourse to the Spirit, which tends toward mental dryness. The goal is not mere warm fuzzies, nor erudition, the goal is for the encounter with God's word to challenge one's whole person and for that encounter to bear fruit in life. Those who practiced *lectio divina* often stayed with the same passage as long as they needed to put it into practice. For obedient action (not accumulation of quantity of knowledge) was the measure of whether one had given the Word of God its proper place of authority in one's life. It is those who actually heed Christ's words and do them whose house is built upon the rock (Matt 7:24).

Practice: *The Beatitudes from Matthew 5:1-10 is perhaps the best known and least believed or lived passage of Jesus' teaching. Using this passage, follow the three readings of lectio divina as a group. As you try out this approach, following the instructions for each reading and each reflection, record your impressions in your journal. Note especially if anything shifts in your understanding as a result of the shift in your posture and vice versa.*

Questions: Poverty & Authority

Guides
Lectio Divina
What do you find compelling about the *lectio divina* approach to reading scripture?

How have changes in your posture changed access to and impact of God's word in your life?

Companions
So What? Says Who?
What is the current ethos regarding the Bible in spiritual authority?

How difficult do we find it to establish common ground of authority to appeal to when talking to others in our church? in our peer group?

You have heard it said...
Capture a list as a group of "you have heard it said" common beliefs from our culture that Jesus might correct with a "but I say to you..."

Journal
Self Assessment
How would I describe my posture toward God's Word?

What degree of authority do I award it in my life?

What needs to change in this area?

POVERTY & UNKNOWING

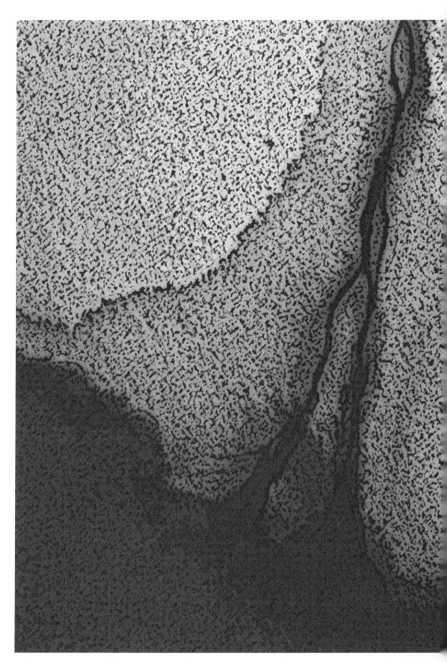

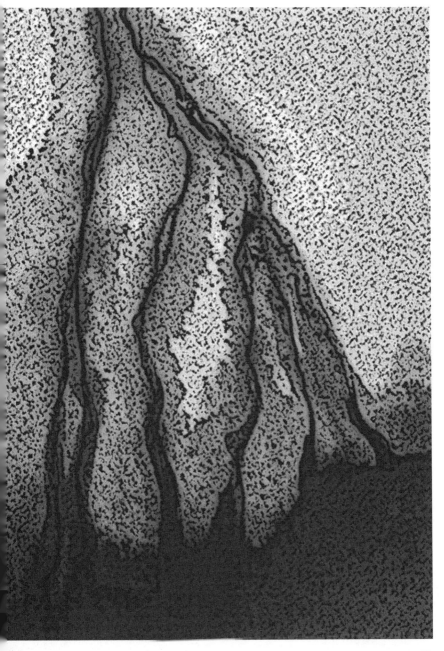

Taking a Bearing

Hey, this isn't fun anymore.

Searching should not be confused with Googling; there is a big difference between a seeker and a surfer. We live in an age that reinforces the expectation of easy change. It seems like everywhere you turn some product or service (a spa, a candy bar) is promising instant wholesale transformation for the taking. Our Christian spiritual expectations mirror the culture at large. We feel disappointed when the half hour worship wasn't effervescent enough to give us a buzz, and we fidget when the biblical insights are not served up from the pulpit in bite-sized bits. We suspect from the headaches that ensue, that perhaps the spiritual equivalent of a diet of soda pop and chocolate bonbons (though very tasty and easy) may cause serious truth decay and malnourish our souls. We are actively being conditioned by our culture to not hunger for better.

One aspect of our culture this journey into poverty immediately challenges is the principle that difficulty means there must be something wrong. We are taught that difficulties, impediments to instant solutions or knowledge, somehow point to some deficiency, if not in ourselves, then in our environment which needs fixing, pronto. People who aren't able to "get" things quickly are slow. So we go through life either pretending we have already got it or flitting here and there, pursuing only what is easy but doesn't satisfy. Scarcity of information used to create some need to engage in pursuit. The immediacy of information today calls to question the value of engaging with truth at all. Why bother wrestling with a truth to *own* it when I can "Wikipedia" it again later when I need to? If the information age has a religion, accessibility is its god. Nothing should be difficult to access. Social media acquires info and big data, and the web puts it within reach of everyone. Increasingly web communities cluster around interest, not age, education, or life experience. This creates a lowest common denominator effect. The 11 year-old, should not be made to feel that any knowledge is out of their reach. This quasi-democratic notion asserts that there is nothing that qualitatively differentiates truth. All content becomes opinion, a matter of taste. Appetite determines interest, and hence, value. In this consumerist worldview, God is not merely dead; he is on the menu.

All content is *pret a manger* (ready to eat), if not actually pre-chewed by marketing machines for us. Why work for knowledge, if there is really no such thing as something better, truer? We are asked to eat our way through religious content in our spiritual life in the same way, to pursue matters of faith almost as a kind of religious consumer entertainment. People are even happy to talk about something hard, like poverty, just so long as it is still entertaining and easy to understand. Even poverty can have pop appeal. But when it crosses the line; people will let you know, "Hey, this isn't fun any more." Depth and complexity are characteristics of poverty that are not so fun. That aching sensation in the frontal cortex, which tokens mental exertion, the discomfort in the gut trying to unknot an unresolved emotion, are conditions we are strongly advised to avoid. We are falsely told there is no need to wrestle with the Spirit of God, refusing to let go like Jacob until he blesses us and perhaps wounds us in the process (Gen 32:24). We are falsely informed that all the truth we need can be found in "The 7 Habits of the Slogan-Driven Life" or whatever the latest Christian self-help book is called. This worldview of easy truth is confirmed because we lose our confidence and give up long before we can put the lie to the test and discover if there are things that don't come easily. The irony is that it is the very posture of a consumer of truth (trying something on, buying only what we want) that prevents us from seeking truth beyond the bullet point version, or experiencing anything beyond our weak spiritual appetites. How can we gain any deeper truth if our tolerance for complexity is so low?

Mother Teresa confided to her confessor that once her calling to Calcutta was confirmed she ceased to hear from God in the intimate, personal, straightforward way she was used to growing up. She could not understand how God who had seemed so tangibly present to her in clear dialogue with her heart could seem so distant and (except for a five week period in 1959), feel completely absent. It caused her great trouble and spiritual doubt, but she continued to follow the last clear orders she was given by God throughout her whole life, long after the newness of the experience was gone, in fact, long after everything was gone except the grinding repetitiveness of poverty all around her, mirrored in the utter poverty she experienced within. We tend to think that the saints of God have some special light, have their way paved, have a direct line to hear God clearly all the time. We mistakenly think that faith means always seeing the truth simply and always knowing what to do. Mother Teresa is one among many that teach us that clarity and simplicity are not guaranteed. She found consolation, by learning to discern the face of God in those suffering ones whom she served, "Christ in our hearts, Christ in the poor we meet, Christ in the smile we give and in the smile that we receive."[1] She also knew something of the fellowship with Jesus Christ in his feelings of confusion and abandonment when he cried "*Eloi, Eloi, lama sabachthani*" (Matt 27:46). We know from the Psalm Christ was quoting in that heart-wrenching cry that the Father never actually abandoned the

---

[1] Van Biema, David "Mother Teresa's Crisis of Faith" *Time* (August 23, 2007)

Son (Psalm 22:24). However, that does not change his complete sharing in our human experience of feeling alone in the dark. Will we still trust and follow hard after truth, when things are not clear, when the sun passes behind a cloud?

Charting a Course
Read James 1:1-8.

The first chapter of James is a passage packed with many things relevant for our journey. We will spend some more time on the specific passages on poverty later on, but first, take note of verses two through eight. They address very pointedly the expectations of the journey we are discussing.

"Consider it pure joy, my brothers, whenever you face trials of many kinds, because you know that the testing of your faith develops perseverance. Perseverance must finish its work so that you may be mature and complete, not lacking anything. If any of you lacks wisdom, he should ask God, who gives generously to all without finding fault, and it will be given to him. But when he asks, he must believe and not doubt, because he who doubts is like a wave of the sea, blown and tossed by the wind. That man should not think he will receive anything from the Lord; he is a double minded man, unstable in all he does."

It is almost as if James were writing in answer to the comment, "It shouldn't be so hard." He responds by stating that the difficulty is not only to be expected but embraced with joy. Hard things are the means by which you prove what you believe is true. This of course is counter intuitive, because everyone assumes that if you are favored by God, you can prove that by how good your life and the world is. If he is good and strong, then the proof of that is smooth sailing, right? Wrong. If all you see is sunshine how will you ever know if your raincoat works in those conditions? God wants us to grow up and have what we really need. But one of the first things we lack is wisdom. We were just corrected two seconds ago on one of our childish preconceptions of how the universe rewards those who love God with freedom from hardship. That was such a comforting delusion that God's favorites are rich and safe and warm, and only the evil suffer. Without that black and white simplification, now how are we supposed to interpret what we see? What we see is certainly crying out for some explanation.

James points us in the right direction. Ask God. Don't go through your life in spiritual infancy because you think you've got it all figured out. If you stay there, you'll never get true wisdom. Step out in faith, and ask God to explain. However, we have to start with what we don't know in order to receive wisdom in the areas we lack it. That sounds like an obvious point, but don't miss the trade off. It is as if God is saying, "First, open your hand. Yes, drop altogether, what you think you have in your hand already. Look there, see it was nothing, dust, lint, empty. Now close your eyes and hold out your hand so I can give you something real." We needn't be afraid about what we don't know or of admitting ignorance. We all know about the discomfort inherent in the state of unknowing, standing there in the dark with our hand held out. Our faith rests in the God who is not stingy when it comes to wisdom. He is not going to play a trick. He also never dishes it out based on how smart or right we are. The only condition is to receive it in faith. Oh and by the way, receiving doesn't mean taking the gift with the intention of returning it if we don't like it! Ask only if you mean it.

The child receiving with eyes closed is an image of the posture of poverty. The empty hand tokens an admission of the lack of wisdom that James speaks of. The closed eyes spell out the trust in God, rather than self. It is incredibly uncomfortable to not understand and still be OK with that, to not race in your mind to solve things or figure it all out. We want to open our eyes and peek. Starting with an empty hand not only makes us learners toward other people (which makes a thousand things better), it puts us in the right attitude to receive Divine wisdom. If we trust God enough, we will close our eyes (a sign of the voluntary privation of physical sight as a source of knowledge). If we always know or can figure anything out, then we do not need to go to God as the source. We are playing God in the attribute of his omniscience.

In our original sin, we sought to be the ones who could know and discern good and evil for ourselves, which by definition seeks to displace God's role as the source of all light. When Christ then made a way for us, he defined the path as difficult and narrow for the very reason that it was by faith. What is difficult about the Gospel is not its intellectual complexity, but its requirement that we shed all notions of having attained or grasped it ourselves. It is a gift. All spiritual wisdom follows suit. You will never receive wisdom if you don't ask God, and you will never ask if you don't think you need to, because you have easy access to knowledge in and through yourself.

We need a healthy skepticism about our knowledge. The apostle Paul once said that "he is resolved to know nothing save Christ and him crucified." That is bold unknowing. And there is a reason we are advised to "Trust in the Lord with all your heart, and lean not on your own understanding" (Prov 3:5). Our knowledge can't be trusted. Contrary to popular thought, knowledge is not morally neutral. All the knowers are corrupt. Trust only the righteous, all-knowing Judge in his assessment.

The biblical witness has also underscored three important (but neglected) epistemologies, which are the terms of appropriate knowledge of poverty, namely, faith, hope, and love. If we think we are able to know some mystery hidden in God by some other way, we kid ourselves. Some people think of faith as the epistemology of last resort, to which they appeal when they can't know in some other (better) way, first. As a result, we have relegated faith to the margins of knowledge, rather than give it its rightful place as a central epistemology for understanding everything in the created order. Nothing can be fully or rightly known apart from knowing it in its Creator. We are told that the epistemology of faith is "the substance of things hoped for", and that it "comes by hearing the Word of God." Biblically informed faith is not just for religious material but a necessary lens for understanding every aspect of life.

The way hope perceives and interprets the world is also unique. Hope has the capacity to imagine an in-breaking Kingdom, different from the world of injustices we see with our eyes, and to believe that unseen promises are more true, more substantial a description of the way things are now, should be, and will be. And the greatest and most enduring of epistemologies, Love, has the capacity to shape the relationships between the knower and the known and to transform both in the process. Love is not a static way of knowing, but rather has a direction. Love seeks to know the world in the context of the deepening embrace of God's reconciliation in Christ. Consequently, to know in love is to become a participant in Jesus' redemption of all people and things. Gone is the posture of distant observer and critic. Gone is the notion that a thing in itself, its make up, is its most fundamental identity. All things are what they are in their most fundamental relationship with their Creator. Not only are we unable to know the world as it is apart from Love, we are told that those who do not love, do not know God either.

There is a lot of wisdom God wants to give us on this journey, which requires a shift in our worldview. That will be harder to shift if we are clutching to it tightly. Mirroring James' audience's preconceptions of suffering and blessing, our view of plenty and poverty tends to fit into categories, the boxes our culture has created to break apart and contain such hazardous material. We are quick to revert to those categories when we feel lost. They are nice boxes; they bring comfort, but they are not "the truth, the whole truth and nothing but the truth, so help me, God." If we intentionally restrain our habit of mind (to reduce in order to comprehend), if we let go of what we think we know, we can close our eyes and open our hand to God the source of all wisdom. We may find he has simply given us his hand.

Ancient Roadmaps
It is a spiritual discipline worth practicing to stay in a posture of unknowing. Humbling of the mind to receive from God, is a key element of the Christian contemplative tradition.

The Discipline of Unknowing

We need to pursue God and truth in intellectual humility. The 14th century English author of the spiritual treatise, *The Cloud of Unknowing*, is representative of this tradition. His work provided an important corrective on scholastic traditions that suggested the proper response to complexity and Divine mystery was to apply greater reason and study harder.

He writes, "When I say darkness, I mean a lacking of knowing...and for this reason it is not called a cloud of the air, but a cloud of unknowing that is betwixt thee and thy God. It is a dark mist which seemeth to be between thee and the light thou aspirest to...the mysterious radiance of the Divine Dark, the inaccessible light wherein the Lord is said to dwell, and to which thought with all its struggles cannot attain."

This practice not only takes difficulty of access to Divine wisdom as a given, but teaches the embrace of this cloud of unknowing as characteristic of true pursuit. The shabby substitute paths not only don't deliver truth; they are more likely to mark out "the soft way to Hell."

Reflect on the following examples of errors and remedies the discipline of unknowing addresses.

1. We don't know because we seek other things, not God. Our object of knowledge is wrong. Unknowing rivets our loving attention toward God.

"When thou comest by thyself, think not before what thou shalt do after, but forsake as well good thoughts as evil thoughts, and pray not with thy mouth but listen thee right well. And then if thou aught shalt say, look not how much nor how little that it be, nor weigh not what it is nor what it meaneth...and look that nothing live in thy working mind but a naked intent stretching into God...Of God himself can no man think. And therefore I would leave all that thing that I can think, and choose to my love that thing that I cannot think."[2]

2. We don't know because we seek God as if he is something else. Our epistemology of knowing God assumes he is like other things we "possess" in our self-referential, self-justifying knowledge. Unknowing allows us the humility to know by *being known* by God.

---

[2] Anonymous *The Cloud of Unknowing* (ca 1375 AD), Foreword by Evelyn Underhill (Kessing, 2010). See also Kierkegaard, Soren *Purity of Heart Is to Will One Thing* (Harper One, 1994)

"Therefore swink and sweat in all that thou canst and mayst, for to get thee a true knowing and a feeling of thyself as thou art; and then I trow that soon after that, thou shalt have a true knowing and a feeling of God as he is."

3. We don't know because we seek God through artificial means. Our religion falsely leads us to believe that we can attain to God by means of ritual or study itself. Unknowing puts us under the grace of revelation.

"For silence is not God, nor speaking is not God; fasting is not God, nor eating is not God; loneliness is not God, nor company is not God; nor yet any of all the other two such contraries. He is hid between them, and may not be found by any work of thy soul, but all only by love of thine heart. He may not be known by reason, he may not be gotten by thought, nor concluded by understanding; but he may be loved and chosen with the true lovely will of thine heart."

Practice: *One way we can embrace the cloud of unknowing and know God by love rather than by intellect, is to practice the Jesus prayer used in spiritual formation in the Orthodox Christian tradition:*[3]

Lord Jesus Christ, Son of God, have mercy on me, a sinner.

We pray the prayer as the honest cry of our hearts, like those wretched, poor, broken, leprous, blind, lame ones along the roadside who called out to the same Lord of Mercy during his earthly ministry. In this practice, repetition is employed to displace other forms of petition and the thoughts that crowd our apparent knowing. We repeat it until such time that the truth of the mercy of God is experienced, not merely thought. For a whole day the prayer should be said out loud, without ceasing, until it becomes rhythmic like breathing. On the second day one can progress to saying it silently. Eventually, it will become a recurrent thought of the heart and a reflexive form of the soul as it reaches towards God in love.

Lord Jesus Christ, Son of God, have mercy on me, a sinner.
Lord Jesus Christ, Son of God, have mercy on me, a sinner.
Lord Jesus Christ, Son of God, have mercy on me, a sinner.
Lord Jesus Christ, Son of God, have mercy on me, a sinner.
Lord Jesus Christ, Son of God, have mercy on me, a sinner.
Lord Jesus Christ, Son of God, have mercy on me, a sinner.
Lord Jesus Christ, Son of God, have mercy on me, a sinner.

---

[3] Anonymous *The Way of the Pilgrim: and the Pilgrim Continues His Way*, Ed. Walter J. Ciszek (Image Classics, 2009).

Questions: Poverty & Unknowing

Guides

Babes in the Wood

We are forced to enter every new culture as children. Suddenly, we don't know most things. How has cross-cultural adjustment aided in your acceptance of unknowing?

What value have you found in remaining in a cloud of unknowing?

Companions

Easy Access

Why do we think understanding things should not be difficult?

In what areas of our life and education do we see the temptation of easy access?

No idea, and that's OK.

Where are areas we are hard on ourself or others for not "getting it", not being "woke" enough, or having things figured out?

Journal

Unknowing

Have I seen the need to know, to reduce to categories, to solve riddles and puzzles in my own thoughts recently?

What can I do to recognize the tendency for quick answers and explanations?

How can I try to be OK remaining in unknowing longer?

Cramming

How tired am I from trying to cram knowledge and understand this new environment?

Am I open to receiving (as a gift) wisdom that is beyond my capacity?

POVERTY & DISPARITY

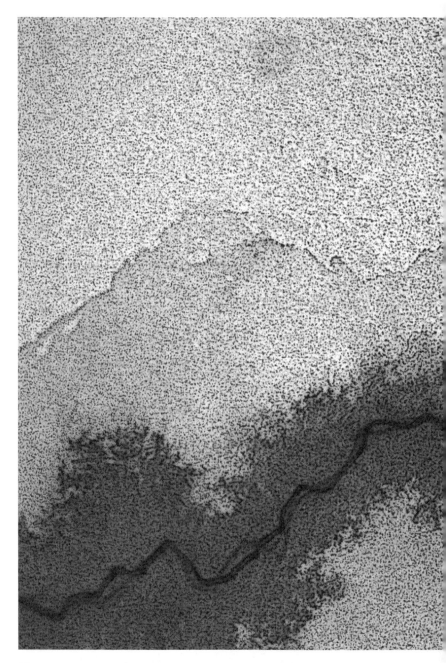

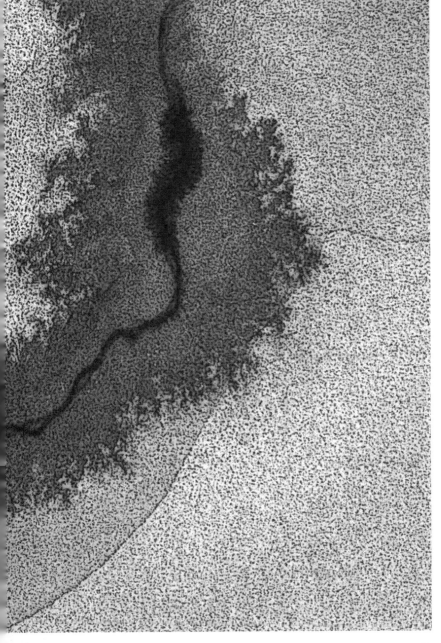

Taking a Bearing

In terms of material goods, we have so much, and they have so little. How should we respond to being rich?

People use the word poverty to denote many different things and degrees of want or lack. One of the first things that leaving one of the wealthier countries in the world does is blow away the contextual framework for one's definition of poverty. Suddenly felt and not just heard, the magnitude of disparity between rich and poor literally makes the mind reel at the injustice of it. It is compounded by the magnitude of disparity between countries and regions, which acts as a multiplier of distance between those living large and those barely living.

The widening gap between incomes within countries like the U.S. is an accelerating trend wrenching at the very fabric of that society. From 2013 to 2015 the richest 14 individuals in the U.S. saw a $157 billion increase in their personal wealth.[1] Their two year earnings was equal to the total wealth of the bottom 40%. The top 1% earns 40 times more than the bottom 90%.

We are further made to consider that average annual income in the twenty richest nations is $27,591, whereas the poorest average only $211. That is a ratio of 131:1 up from 30:1 in 1960 and about 9:1 at the beginning of the twentieth century. From 2016 the top 1% of all people in the world owned half of the entire world's assets and wealth, and the poorest half of the population owned less than 1% of the wealth. So what happens to the incredible wealth creation we keep hearing about in the global economy? It appears to be concentrating in fewer hands at an accelerating rate. The rich are getting richer, and the poor are getting poorer.

In 2002, an online game, Everquest, was ranked the 77th richest country in the world (richer than Bulgaria).[2] The game hosted a virtual country, Norrath, which had a higher gross national product per capita ($2,226), than China and India. That means people are spending more money to buy fake goods inside fake worlds than entire countries spend on real goods for real citizens in the real world. This expenditure on entertainment is a picture of how our money can get trapped in artificial environments and fail to get to where it is desperately needed, where it could do some real good.

However, these facts and statistics don't sink in until we step out and see, or feel, how much all things are out of all proportion. It is like landing on the moon and suddenly realizing that you don't weigh as much as you do

---

[1] Hardoon, Deborah "Wealth: Having it All and Wanting More" (Oxfam International: January, 2015).

[2] "Virtual Kingdom Richer than Bulgaria" BBC News (March 29, 2002).

back home. It is an experience that is deeply disruptive to one's sense of equilibrium to find that the system of weights and measures one is using for wealth and poverty, like gravity, is not universal. This is why NGOs use adjectives like abject, extreme, and absolute, to try to give some sense of proportion to poverty for people who, living in a Costco-sized world, have no idea of the scale and intensity of hunger much of the world is suffering.

There is poor, and then there is not-knowing-where-any-future-resource-is-coming-from poor. The most troubling thing is, that once we've readjusted our measures to an international reality, we are forced to the uncomfortable conclusion that we are not the underdog. Our minds race to compare, to assure ourselves that we are not so rich, but we see the disparity now first-hand, and we feel the distance of the category those in extreme poverty (living on less than $1.90 per day) place us in. They see us as "the rich" as much as we tend to see them as "the poor." We cannot escape the fact that compared to most, in economic terms, we are rich.

Processing this does not mean neutral observation of the fact. That is impossible. The injustice of unequal distribution of goods in spite of equal human worth is made clear, and we cannot just accept it as a fact of life and move on. For we are part of the disparity equation. Is it possible that we live in such a complex, wicked world that we contribute to disparity without setting out to do so? Guilt causes some to give up all hopes of ever doing justice and others to prescribe simplistic rules for avoiding injustice. Thankfully, the Lord of love doesn't let us off the hook so easily.

Looking at the scale and pace of growing disparity of material wealth in the church and world today, how does anything but extreme generosity and radical redistribution to those at the bottom reflect the true impetus, direction and momentum of the Gospel? With the Spirit of Christ in us, how can we not run down hill like water to fill up the lowest places?

Charting a Course
Read Acts 4:31-5:11.
The New Testament is full of Christ's call to respond to those in need. There are many different responses to poverty, some good models, some bad. If you suspect the Bible will reward us with an easy, static answer to how to do justly, you are mistaken. Jesus spoke into a world that already had such well-structured systems for right living, including prescriptions for giving alms and tithing. From the beginning it was apparent that he would be demanding more, "Except your righteousness exceed the righteousness of the Scribes and Pharisees, ye shall in no wise enter into the kingdom of heaven." (Matt 5:20).

"Ah, so you want us to give more?"

"No, no, it is not a matter of quantity. Verily I say unto you, That this poor widow hath cast more in, than all they which have cast into the treasury: For all they did cast in of their abundance; but she of her want did cast in all that she had, even all her living" (Mark 12:43).

"Ah, so you want us to give a bigger proportion? What percentage should we increase our tithe by?"

"No, no, don't you remember what happened with Zacchaeus? What did he do? He gave half of his possessions and restored four times what he cheated" (Luke 19:8).

"Ah, so you want us to give 50%?"

"No, no, you see that rich, young ruler leaving, dejected? What did I ask him to do? To sell all he had and give to the poor and follow me" (Matt 19:16).

"Ah, so you want us to sell 100% of our possessions, cash it in, and give it away? That would certainly feed a lot of people. Take that ointment that lady broke all over your feet, now that could have been sold, and..."

"No, no, I don't want you to think of it like that at all. It isn't a matter of cash value. She was obedient, and she did not hold back at all, but you are still measuring, still calculating. It is not the measure of the thing that awards it value to me. If anyone has material possessions and sees his brother in need but has no pity on him, how can the love of God be in him?" (1 John 3:17).

"Ah, so you want us to give whenever we are asked up to the point that we have no more. We should give till it hurts."

"No, no, I am not interested in the pain of your sacrifice. And though I bestow all my goods to feed the poor, and though I give my body to be burned, and have not charity, it profiteth me nothing" (1 Cor 13:3).

"Ah, so you want us to love them; that's more important than giving."

"No, no, My little children, let us not love in word, neither in tongue; but in deed and in truth" (1 John 3:18).

In Acts 4:31- 5:11 we see the followers of Christ finally getting it, and then...not. The Spirit of God filled them with such love that they no longer counted what was theirs as theirs. They no longer calculated. They were moved in love to sell their possessions and give the proceeds to the common good. Significantly, they did not insist on being on the redistribution committee based on how much they gave. They laid it at the Apostles' feet for them to redistribute according to everyone's need. One example was Barnabas whom Love compelled to sell some real estate and give all the proceeds to the community.

Pretty soon, it was hard to find anyone who lacked in their community. But there were some who mistook form for substance. From the outside it looks like the holy thing to do is to join the bandwagon, sell some real estate, make a contribution and receive kudos from God and the community. If you start by thinking it is all about real estate, you very quickly can identify the loopholes. We can follow the form exactly, if that is all that is required and still avoid it costing us so much. "What they don't know won't hurt them; they should be grateful we give anything at all."

Peter's rebuke of Ananias is telling, why has Satan filled your heart to lie and keep back part? What it points to is our desire to be justified. The need of our brothers and sisters sets up an obligation of love. We do not want to be perceived as unjust; so our first thought is to find a way to avoid the negative perception, to keep up appearances. And why not hold back? It is the more balanced thing to do. You never know when I might need that, and it is really up to me to adjudicate on who really needs what, especially *my* needs. Peter asks him if it was not his property and his cash from the sale. He was free to do with it whatever he wanted.

Priscilla and Aquila had a property they kept and which served as a church and a place of great help for Apollos and Paul (Acts 18,1 Cor 16). So it is not about keeping it or selling it. It is *so not* about real estate. If he was not moved by God's love to give it all, then why would he pretend he was? Did he think his mockery benefitted the community or impressed anyone? Did he really think God was fooled and not insulted by the imitation? His conspiracy dragged the love of the Spirit of God (who manifests the gift of his presence in generosity) into the mud and reduced the demands of love to a property trade. So the whole world would know the difference between show and substance, and seek the latter in the Spirit, the couple dies. Faking the generosity of the Spirit is a serious crime in the Christian community.

So, neither selling a possession (Barnabas) or not (Aquila) is the measure. Sometimes their giving it up, sometimes their keeping it to use for God in other ways is good. So what makes a gift good? The giver? Not. The shape of the gift? Not. The proportion or regularity of giving? Not. It is precisely the notion of merit and measuring love that poisons it. The only measure of our response to needs in an unjust world is obedience. It is not for us to assess the utility of the Will of God. To do so reasserts our own will as judges of justice. Who are we to assume we can discern his world better than he? And the fact that it is just plain invisible from the outside what is sacrifice and what is obedience, should prevent us from judging the actions or inactions of others as well.

""But divine compassion, the infinite *unconcern* which takes thought only of those that suffer, and not in the least of one's self, and which with absolute unconcern takes thought of all that suffer: that will always seem to men only a kind of madness, and they will ever be puzzled whether to laugh or to weep about it...For men are willing enough to practice sympathy and self-denial, are willing enough to strive for wisdom, etc.; but they wish themselves to determine the standard and to have that read: "to a certain degree." They do not wish to do away with all these splendid virtues. On the contrary, they want—at a bargain and in all comfort—to have the appearance and name of practicing them. Truly divine compassion is therefore necessarily the victim so soon as it shows itself in this world."[3]

It is not about extremes or balance. It is not about what justice should look like. Justice is quite simply, whatever God asks of us. And he measures right to the heart. The thought of faking generosity or offering our own "prudent" alternative or following a socially constructed substitute for obedience should make us think "Ananias" and tremble. Christ offers a new freedom from our own self-referential and self-justifying measurements of justice through simple, Spirit-led obedience.

Ancient Roadmaps
Fasting is a very old spiritual discipline intended to restore our relationship of God-dependency and thereby to restore relationships of justice with others.

The Discipline of Fasting
It is interesting for our study of poverty that one of the oldest known rites of spiritual devotion has to do with abstention from food. Many religions practice fasting as a ritual means of either overcoming the passions or persuading their deities to get what they want (roughly the spiritual equivalent of a child threatening to hold its breath until it gets its way). Because of the hardship involved, the practice has often come to be seen as an ascetic virtue, which separates the committed from the rest. Like all spiritual disciplines it should never become an end in itself. However, abuse is no excuse to avoid it. Christ rebuked those who did it for show or self-righteousness or tried to earn something by it, but he also modeled

[3] Kierkegaard, Soren, "The Preparation for a Christian Life" in *Selections from the Writings of Kierkegaard*, Trans Lee M. Hollander (New York: Doubleday Anchor, 1960), 208.

its true practice to his disciples who practice it as an integral part of their life of prayer and communion with God. So what should fasting be? Isaiah 58:4-6 spells it out:

"Behold, ye fast for strife and debate, and to smite with the fist of wickedness: ye shall not fast as ye do this day, to make your voice to be heard on high. Is it such a fast that I have chosen, a day for a man to afflict his soul? Is it to bow down his head as a bulrush, and to spread sackcloth and ashes under him? Wilt thou call this a fast, and an acceptable day to the LORD? Is not this the fast that I have chosen, to loose the bands of wickedness, to undo the heavy burdens, and to let the oppressed go free, and that ye break every yoke? Is it not to deal thy bread to the hungry, and that thou bring the poor that are cast out to thy house? when thou seest the naked, that thou cover him; and that thou hide not thyself from thine own flesh? Then shall thy light break forth as the morning..."

Fasting is not about getting God to listen. It is not to cover up your injustices or guilt. It is not for self-affliction. It is not about outward signs of humility. Ashes only mean anything, if they are accompanied by a contrition that matches the mortality they signify. Bowing one's knees only means anything, if it is accompanied by humility that bends us on the inside. If going without food reminds you of your brother's incessant hunger, if your heightened sense of physical dependency reminds you that you are not superior, that you are your brother's equal and have no special right or merit to feel more full than they, if abstaining from food moves you to not only abstain from injustice, but makes your desire to relieve your brother's suffering eclipse your desire to relieve your own hunger, then that is fasting. Fasting shouldn't end in more inward focus, but restore perspective and proportion to needs and wants, hopefully resulting in taking ourselves far less (and others, far more) seriously.[4]

Practice: *Take a day to fast as a physical reminder of poverty. Start by asking God when he would have you fast and for how long. Ask if there is something, or someone which God wants you to focus on while you fast. If you are new to it, start with a meal before fasting for a full 24 hours. Check in at several times during the day, especially at meal times. Journal about what God is speaking and where he is leading you in your understanding of poverty through this discipline.*

---

[4] Pattison, Bonnie L. *Poverty in the Theology of John Calvin. Princeton Theological Monograph Series* (Eugene: Wipf & Stock, 2006).

Questions: Poverty & Disparity

Guides
I am rich?
What things in particular stand out in your mind to remind you that you are economically rich?

What are some examples of how material inequality in the world has been made personal for you?

Companions
Disparity
What are our impressions of income disparity between our home and vulnerable contexts, and how have we been processing that so far?

Response
What are some of the rule-based responses to poverty we've experienced in our churches and Christian organizations?

Journal
Disparity
How should I respond to being economically rich?

Obedience
Are there examples where I know I have been disobedient to what I know God wants of me and just did something to keep up appearances?

POVERTY & PROSPERITY

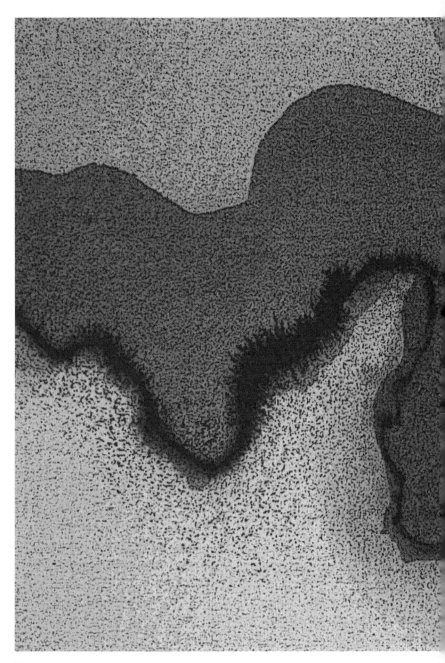

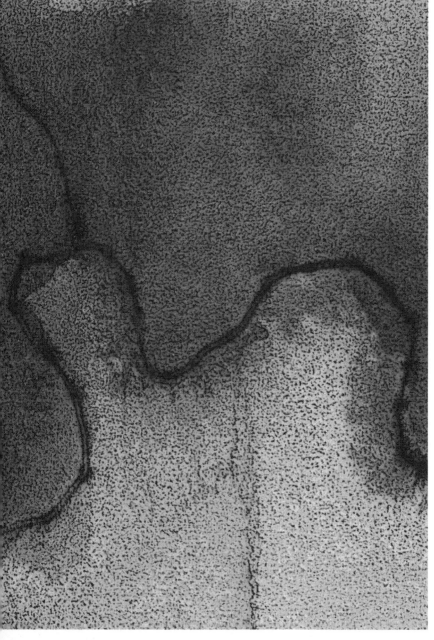

Taking a Bearing

Do the rich and the poor deserve what they have?

The prosperity gospel is something lurking in the subconscious of rich Christians that needs rooting out. The true premise is that God cares about our physical condition as well as our spiritual condition; he cares about redeeming the whole person. However, the false conclusion is that material prosperity in this world is something that God guarantees us, and that in fact, our prosperity is a measure of our favor with and faith in God. The converse is not far behind, namely, that those individuals, communities, and cultures who lack material prosperity, also lack faith and or the favor of God. It is likely they are under some Divine judgment.

It boggles the mind how people can think this way with a Bible open in front of them, but the prosperity gospel is no small movement. Recent statistics suggest that over 60% of people claiming to be evangelicals in the U.S. agree with the tenets of the prosperity gospel. And we are all susceptible to the seduction of imbibing the American dream as theology. Prosperity theology claims (contrary to all warnings of Christ) that the pursuit of riches, which our culture enthrones, is blessed. It helps the guilt of prosperity to believe the lie that our wealth is God's agenda or goal. Importantly for our study, this insidious set of lies can infect how we interpret and engage with physical poverty. What is the great advantage of seeing poverty first-hand, if the lens through which we see is bent?

When we see poverty do we immediately look for what must be wrong with that culture? I mean, what kind of culture doesn't see the absolute necessity of indoor plumbing? How messed up do you have to be to not be able to manage that? We easily fall into the role of Job's friends (Job 4:7). Instead of identifying ourselves with and sharing in the misery of others, we distance ourselves in judgment. And we sin by ascribing to God a one-to-one, mechanistic relationship with his universe, blessing for the good and smart, cursings for the evil and ignorant.

We should ask ourselves why we try to figure out what "makes" the poor more deserving of the blight they are suffering. Many latch on to the notion that they (or their ancestors) must have done something really morally reprehensible. Some of the more public proponents of this moral mechanistic worldview (which is more animistic than Christian) have attributed the various sufferings we witness (HIV, earthquakes, tsunami, illiteracy, famine) to specific spiritual sins. C. S. Lewis noted in his essay on historicism, that when we interpret natural disasters like earthquakes, hurricanes, floods, and famines today as an act of God's judgment, or when we communicate that we believe the political woes of particular citizens in oppressed countries are somehow deserved, we are not only dangerously claiming prophetic powers, but we are dishonoring Christ by attributing to him the behavior of pagan deities.[1] This practice is as detestable as fortune-telling with blood and chicken bones.

Christ took both aspects of the prosperity gospel head on. Responding to this method of simplistic fault-finding to explain tragedy, he went right to the root of our self-protecting delusion. "And Jesus answering said unto them, Suppose ye that these Galileans were sinners above all the Galileans, because they suffered such things? I tell you, Nay: but, except ye repent, ye shall all likewise perish." (Luke 13:2ff). Don't convince yourself that the suffering of others reinforces your special moral status. They are no worse than you, and you are under the same original curse.

Christ dismantles the other side of that worldview as well, namely, that physical prosperity always corresponds to God's favor. In contrast, he makes audacious claims like "the poor are (already) blessed." The poor have an advantage over the rich (who need to come to God through absolute poverty anyway). The poor are ahead of the rich on the path to the Kingdom of God. So which is the curse and which the blessing?

In every generation, there are particular enemies of the Gospel. In our generation, the Gospel must testify against the idolatries of self and pragmatism, economic reductionism, and certainly, the lie of the prosperity gospel. Our best testimony against these is to do justly, love mercy, and walk humbly with our God (Micah 6:8).

Charting a Course
Read Revelation 3:14-22.

"Who you callin' poor?" There is perhaps no passage of scripture more unsettling, more disruptive to traditional notions of the blessing of prosperity and the curse of poverty than the letter to the church at Laodicea. There is no doubt from the outset that this church is in trouble. There is no pretending that vomiting is a sign of God's favor (the King James version with "spewing" seems mild compared to the more visceral Greek). It is the only place in the Bible this image is attributed to God. His displeasure apparently has something to do with their spiritual temperature. The church was not going to reject God and his demands outright, that would be cold. Neither would it embrace them passionately; that was a little too hot for their tastes. They had settled on a Goldilocks porridge version of their faith. The church had fallen prey to the common curse of mitigating the demands of love by a kind of law of averages. They preferred a more balanced, happy medium to the demands of the Gospel.

---

[1] Lewis, C. S. "Historicism" in *Fern Seed and Elephants: And Other Essays on Christianity* (New York: Collins, 1989), 44ff.

Furthermore, they had convinced themselves that everything was fine. In fact, to all outward appearances, they were doing very well indeed.

The Great Amen used the very thing they thought was evidence of their health as evidence for their need of healing. This compounded the sobering reality that since they couldn't tell the difference, they must be blind. The church had the attitude that we have need of nothing; we lacked nothing. We do not hunger; We have no poverty. But there was no shortage of poverty in their day. Why did they not own those needs as their own? What kind of mental gymnastics involving "us" and "them" are necessary to get to "we are fine?" It should be an obvious first sign of departure from the love of the Gospel that they saw themselves as separate from those in physical poverty and exempt from the shared suffering of the whole body of Christ.

But Christ wanted to challenge more than that. He contradicts the very criteria of their self-assessment. So you think you're rich. I wouldn't be so sure about that. I say you are wretched, miserable, poor, blind, and naked. The people of Laodicea knew very well what prosperity meant. In this provincial city of banking, wool and medicine, prosperity was easily discerned. It meant having enough saved up to never be in need, being well-clothed and in good health. They were a model city of self-sufficiency. They even rebuilt after a devastating earthquake destroyed the town in 60 AD.[2] This they did with their own resources and without help from the emperor. They took care of themselves, they were self-sufficient even in crisis. The parallel with the church's attitude toward God today is not easy to miss.

However, the way in which the True Witness describes them is their worst nightmare, the wretched, impoverished, helpless condition they built all their wealth infrastructure to prevent. This condition you seek to avoid with a life well-buffered from want, you epitomize in my eyes already. He called them poor. His remedy must have cut them to the quick. Trade your poverty for true riches. He called the church to make an exchange, a particularly poignant analogy for a church in one of the premier commercial capitals of the day. He is basically saying that you think you may be rich where you come from, but your currency is no good here. You are in my Kingdom now, and that other money standard has no value.

During the Asian economic crisis of the 1990s many people experienced the sudden devaluation of their currency in the global economy. God sends a message that is even more devastating. Your riches have zero

---

2 Tacitus *The Annals* 14:27.

worth. My currency is based on the gold standard, and only the purest gold refined by fire is worth anything. If you try to use your "riches" of material wealth in my Kingdom you are like those poor miserable, naked, blind wretches you avoid in your world. There has to be some kind of exchange for this to work for you, and good thing for you, I am prepared to exchange what is worthless for things of real value. How could a person with good business sense pass up this kind of offer? Once again, God is asking us to hand over to him what we have in our hands, not because it is as precious as we think it is, but because unless we do, we cannot receive what we need from him. How can we comprehend, let alone begin to appropriate the unspeakable riches of God's grace, if we are still working on an old, defunct system of currency? Christ then called them to repent and be zealous. There is a double pun here, for zealous comes from the same root word as hot and means to have warmth of feeling for something, to passionately seek after some good one doesn't yet possess. The adjective is usually applied to a covetous person, and here it is like saying, "your riches are no good, and even your covetousness is weak. Become very zealous, greedy, for real wealth."

The image of this visceral reaction from God to our economics can leave little doubt about how he feels when we make milk-toast of the demands of his Gospel. It is also very telling that the area where the church reveals its true spiritual condition and perhaps identifies a root spiritual poverty is in its attitudes toward material riches and poverty. The Gospel isn't about tweaking an otherwise OK values system here and there; it entails the complete replacement of the world's values with Kingdom values. Everything is set on its head. Only in reference to Kingdom values can we say with conviction "Let the brother of low degree rejoice in that he is exalted: But the rich, in that he is made low" (James 1:9ff).

Ancient Roadmaps
For some, the means to owning a spirit of poverty was initiated through a formal vow of poverty in the context of a spiritual community.

The Discipline of Renunciation
When seeking to understand renunciation, it is very easy to write off the practices of the monastic tradition as empty asceticism or extreme legalism. Adherence to an institutional response certainly should not be seen as a substitute for heart obedience. However, the two are not incompatible any more than love and vows of marriage are incompatible. Sometimes submission to our spiritual community's interpretation of the demands of obedience can also avoid personal subjectivity in our own interpretation of and response to poverty. Especially when our popular

interpretation seems to depart from the spirit of the New Testament, we should enquire how other Christians in other times have responded.

Poverty movements (in so far as they have testified against idolizing wealth and have recalled those ensnared in prosperity to the heart of God) have proven a powerful tool of God's renewal of the church across the ages. This study wants to present those Christian traditions in such a way that we can learn from any earnest effort in the history of the church to own and end poverty. One such sign, poverty as a vow (along with chastity and obedience vows) has been one of the most common ingredients of Christian religious orders and communities.

That means that a lot of people across church history have responded to poverty in this way. In the vow of poverty tradition it is clearly stated that poverty is not a virtue, neither is voluntary poverty a spiritual merit. They simply held that Christ's stern warnings against riches and the clear condition of forsaking Mammon for the sole Lordship of Christ were things requiring a commensurate response. Jesus said, "Everyone of you that does not renounce all that he possesses, cannot be my disciple" (Luke 14:33). A vow of poverty reads renunciation to mean formal, public and permanent, like the "forsaking all others" in a public marriage vow. Renunciation requires a higher level of accountability than private commitment and needs to be renewed so that it does not become an empty form. To "renounce all" is taken to include material goods. The meaning is not spiritualized by assuming we can acquire the right attitude without reference to what we actually do with our physical goods.

Some traditions read the most important word to be "possesses." Renunciation means the voluntary giving up of one's rights of possession. Hence what one owns is treated as if one didn't really own it and had no rights to it. There is a freedom offering to God to use what is actually God's rather than treating goods "as if" they were our private property. For others, the phrase "that he possesses" sticks out. The threat of falling in love with riches resides in the selfish uses to which we put our possessions. Renunciation entails the sacrifice of all superfluous personal ends (beyond necessity) that we spend our possessions on. This approach teaches contentment with having only what we need.

Seeing others living (and even flourishing on) far less helps us think honestly about "what we need" really means. This points to the prophetic role the vow of poverty can have to the edification of others, not just as a means to avoid greed as an individual. For God has used the powerful testimony of the poor, and the formerly rich, those who have given up all and have lived joyfully in simplicity, to jar the assumptions and anxieties of the rich. The rich rarely go and see, but God brought those wandering, barefoot types like Francis of Assisi to their very doors to set them free.

Others still, believed the only way to mortify the love of riches was to abandon personal possessions altogether. This was done by transferring all property to the ownership of one's spiritual community and with it all rights to dispose of that property as the community and its leaders saw fit. Not owning anything certainly removes all our rights to do what we want with our possessions. We thereby counter the pride of wealth, the pride of the power of money to give us our own way, by surrendering our choices about how we use possessions to another's will. Renunciation of possessions becomes an act of submissive obedience.

This often put a greater burden and temptation on the leaders of the community who attempted to remove the problem from the community altogether, forbidding not only the individual but community ownership of anything and divesting all rights to those in leadership of the church, outside of the community. That got them off the hook, but didn't remove the problem, only concentrated it elsewhere. A complex legal system eventually evolved to govern treatment of property by the religious orders.

The seriousness with which those in the tradition of the formal vow of poverty treated Christ's warnings about wealth, should give us pause. We tend to assume that we have it under control, and that the answer to how we should respond to Luke 14:33 is pretty straight forward. This is a bad sign, since other gifted and committed Christians struggled long and hard over the response God required of them for obedience and for a testimony to others. In light of this, the phrase "cannot be my disciple" reads less like a prerequisite condition and more like a matter-of-fact statement. You could try to have both, but my friend, it simply cannot be done. What the vow of poverty tradition affirms is that our propensity for the love of riches is an insidious enemy that is hard to beat, and that renunciation, continuing in the spirit of poverty, requires great grace from the God who calls us to that condition. Suddenly renunciation doesn't seem so extreme.

The following list summarizes ways various Christian traditions have interpreted the meaning of "renounce" in different times and contexts.

1. "Renounce all that one has" means chiefly a posture of the heart.
The renunciation refers to an inner motion that forsakes the attachment to and love of one's possessions. This posture craves renewal, as the attachment to possessions tends to return.

2. "Renounce all that one has" means a public act of renunciation.
Similar to a public confession or baptism or marriage, this is a singular "speech act" that shifts one's allegiance from possessions to Christ.

3. "Renounce all that one has" means to renounce one's rights to use his/her possessions as they choose. Those rights are bound to the notion of possession, and in voluntarily giving up one's rights to do with what is theirs, they thereby renounce those possessions. It is like saying it is mine, but I will forego the right to use it, as if it is mine.

4. "Renounce all that one has" means to remove all non-necessary uses of possessions from one's life. It is the impetus to live simply and in contentment with food and raiment. One still owns and controls the possessions, but eliminates any hold it has over one beyond what is needed for life. This tradition has varying ways to determine what is necessary and what is not and seeks to affirm that the fullness of life is very much present with very few necessities.

5. "Renounce all that one has" means to renounce individual property ownership. The renunciation is effected by removing any ownership usually through a vow of poverty. Typically this is facilitated by passing to the community or to an order what used to belong to the individual. In imitation of the early Church in Acts, they freely laid at the Apostle's feet what was theirs, but now by choice, was no longer theirs.

6. "Renounce all that one has" means to renounce any kind of ownership of property in the individual and in the community. The community also cannot own anything in this model and participate in the role of stewards only of what has passed into others' hands. This is clearly an extension of interpretation 5 to undermine the very notion of possession in communities as well as in individuals.

*Practice: Ask yourself in what way might some of these signs inform your own expression of renunciation? Is there something in renunciation that promises freedom by removing what might be impeding a right relationships of shalom (e.g. your relationship with God, your self, with others, with the created order, with your community, and with your society)? To participate in this discipline, practice renunciation of just **one** **possession** in one of the six ways modeled, by giving it up, or handing it over to someone else, or divesting decision making over its use, etc.*

Questions: Poverty & Prosperity

Guides
Prosperity Gospel
What are some examples of the messaging of the prosperity gospel you have seen?

Development
How can development (premised on improvement) avoid the moral and cultural posture of superiority?

Companions
Blessed
Is being materially rich a blessing?

What do we consider evidence of God's favor?

What do we make of the condition of renunciation for discipleship?

Renunciation
How do we read the meaning of renouncing all we possess? Randomly assign the views 1-6 and debate them in a group.

Rights of Possession
We assume the right to do with our property what we want. However, it is one of the conditions of poverty to have limited choices. When is it appropriate to voluntarily limit our choices and give up the rights associated with our possessions for others?

Is there something in our current relationship with what we possess that God is nudging us to renounce?

Journal
God's Favor
It is easy to interpret poverty starting from the premise that others are the ones with needs; whereas I have need of nothing. What are the areas of wretchedness and blindness where God is pointing out my poverty?

POVERTY & HAPPINESS

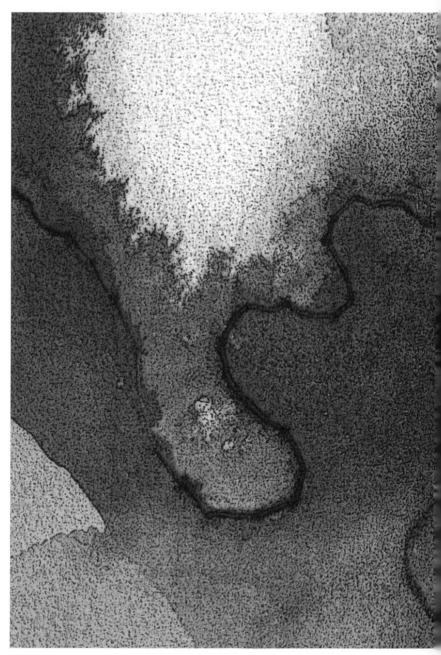

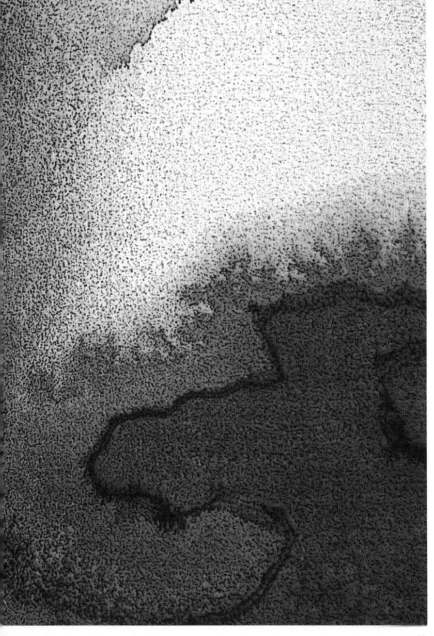

Taking a Bearing
How can people so poor be so happy?
What is even more jarring than an encounter with physical poverty is to find there, the unmistakable, undeniable presence of joy. Talk about a testimony against the delusion of this world's economy. Joy is a slap (or better, a pie) in the face of the "more is more" philosophy of consumerism. We all believe in the importance of happiness. It is written into America's founding documents, that among the inalienable rights endowed by our Creator is the Pursuit of Happiness ("property" in first drafts of the Declaration of Independence). We have been bombarded (through every medium ever invented) with lies about what makes for happiness and where it should be pursued.

Like that board game, "Life", we rarely question the rules of the matrix-reality most people play, which goes by the same name. We just assume that we must be losing so we need to try harder or wait for our luck to change. Whether we have more or we have less, the goal is still acquisition. In that "educational" board game, we acquire a car, an education, a job, a spouse whom we put in the car (recent game versions have upgraded to SUVs), children, which are gender differentiated pink and blue (and which as a kid I used to bite in half to properly reflect their diminutive properties before also sticking them into the car holes, the holes human pegs were designed to fit). We spin the wheel and navigate various turns of fortune to gain the wealth we need to retire in style in some fancy, gated estate. Talk about training in treating everything and everyone as a means to our own financial gain.

The end of "Life" is of course financial security and independence, the ultimate measure of which is owning your own property outright and sitting on a nest egg, big enough, presumably to send your kids off to do the same thing again, only better. Why would we ever question the rules, unless we suddenly saw that there isn't a correlation between acquisition and happiness? We are taught in Christian circles to distinguish between happiness and joy. Sermons on the subject typically start with "happiness has to do with happ-en-ings, but joy is deep within..." Part of me wonders if this half-truth doesn't actually assist our pursuit of material happiness unimpeded, limiting the life encroachment of the spiritual domain, blocking the real truth about joy/happiness from infecting how people live their lives in the "real world."

It also helps to explain away that niggling worry about the absence of joy. The absence of one of the fruits of the Holy Spirit (Gal 5:22) can't be a good sign. "No", we are advised, "Joy is so deep, deep down in the heart, that we shouldn't worry that we fail to register its subterranean activity.

Maybe absence is a good sign." This is all well and good until we have an authentic encounter with joy, unmustered, unfaked, uncontained joy, manifest in one lacking what is supposed to make us happy. There is this spring of living water, not born from the surface, but definitely surfacing. The sermon on the mount declares blessing, happiness and joy to the poor. "In spirit", we hastily add, still trying to keep separate the "spiritual" and "material" worlds. But I must admit I do not know what it means to be poor in spirit without it having some kind of manifestation in one's actual financial records. Christians don't keep two separate sets of books, a set of undeclared accounts for their other life. Divine omniscience kind of undermines that tactic. And whoever heard of a purely interior poverty? Perhaps the same people who are trying to sell a purely interior joy! The connection is deeply unsettling.

M. Scott Peck writes, "Simply seek happiness, and you are not likely to find it. Seek to create and love without regard to your happiness, and you will likely be happy much of the time. Seeking joy in and of itself will not bring it to you. Do the work of creating community, and you will obtain it - although never exactly according to your schedule. Joy is an uncapturable yet utterly predictable side effect of genuine community."[1]

But this still doesn't answer the "so what" about happiness? What difference does joy make? Just think for a moment about the difference between someone trying to get joy by giving something away versus someone giving something away because they have joy. The difference is night and day, but impossible to perceive for those who think about happiness mechanistically. True joy, once realized, is one of the most powerful motivators. This is what is meant by "the joy of the Lord is my strength"; for joy not only provides the impetus but the energy. Doing out of joy is not tedious; our hands are strengthened for even heavy tasks by joy. Christ did what he did, suffering the indignity of the cross all for "the joy set before him", the joy he would experience in winning us to himself. In this case, even the hope of a joy to come was sufficient to carry our Lord through his obedience unto death. In John 15:11 Christ takes that joy he received in the love of the Father, far beyond what happiness the world can give, and he passed that joy to us. It is another reminder that joy is a gift. That Divine origin of our joy becomes most clear to us, when it is there, but there is no-thing, no earthly reason for joy.

---

[1] Peck, M. Scott *The Road Less Travelled* (Touchstone: 25th Anniversary Edition, 2003).

Charting a Course
Read Ecclesiastes 5:8-20.

The best things in life are still free. This passage is an ode to joy but opens on a scene of oppression of the poor and violent perversion of justice. The teacher brutally asks, why are we so shocked and surprised? This is what you get when you combine basic human greed with any hierarchy. The evil and potential for harm multiplies the higher up you look in human government, despite the fact that they are all dependent, even the king, on the same basic resources provided by God through the bounty of the land. No one is above need. The evil (at scale) is not something fundamentally different from what we find in our own hearts. And the root evil must be addressed in the individual heart from whence these exponentially evil injustices spring. The curative is to take a cold hard look at our pursuit of happiness.

Joy cannot be found in riches, which do not satisfy the soul and are not dependable. The book of Ecclesiastes is down-right repetitive on the ephemeral nature of wealth. Financial security is an oxymoron. And so people putting great emotional stock in riches and expending great energy in pursuit of riches as a means to happiness are foolish. In addition, we are warned of a law of diminishing returns at work in those who seek pleasure there. Moreover, a natural limit on acquisition is built into our very creaturely nature. We cannot eat more than one can eat in a day! That is one of the lessons of the manna in the wilderness, the reminder that we are creatures and that we all live day to day by God's providence. The other things we accumulate we can only look at or watch rot. We have no more capacity, and we have no less dependency on God. So what is the point of increasing?

It is also a pitiable condition to miss out on the universal (albeit limited) human joys of life in our work and rest because we have traded them for an illusion of more. We miss out on our heritage from God, and as if that weren't enough, we end up robbing others of the gifts God gives them, and still ending up as bankrupt as we came into this world. Seriously, what profit is the pursuit of profit? But beyond this, Ecclesiastes also spells out a deeper truth, namely, that all good things are totally meaningless apart from the ability to enjoy them.

Such a realization is foreign to us. It boggles our Western minds to think of joy as independent of the objects of our joy. For we have inherited a kind of cause and effect understanding of happiness. Our language betrays us. We use turns of phrase like "what makes you happy", "it causes me great delight". It is no wonder that we find it difficult to get beyond an understanding of joy in and from things.

Even if we come to realize that joy is not caused by money or things, we often err in the other direction and suggest that joy is caused by their absence. The reality is that joy is caused by neither wealth nor poverty. You will not be happier because you have more money or because you choose to have less. Whether you have plenty, or little, the ability to enjoy them is a gift from God. Joy is an independent gift. Joy is not directly proportional to your wealth; neither is it inversely proportional to your wealth. Joy, especially in suffering, is one of the clearest indicators that God grants this gift independent of circumstances.

The sooner we realize the true source of joy in and from God, the sooner we will realize we cannot muster or manufacture it. Though many do not recognize it, no one ever gets joy apart from the One True Joy-giver. The means to finding deeper, enduring joy is to look beyond the gift to the Giver. Joy, happiness, all of it, comes as a gift from the same gracious God who gives life as a gift, independent of any conditions. It makes little sense to talk about anything other than God causing our life. Why do we believe it is different with joy? We are in need of constant reminders that God is the only source of happiness. God gives the ability to enjoy.

One reason that God separates the gift of joy from the other gifts is because he ultimately wants us to recognize that he is the source of joy (in his right hand are pleasures forevermore), and that the Lord himself is the truest object of our joy. He doesn't just want to dish out happiness. He wants to give himself to us, because he knows that it is his person that would bring us our fullest possible joy. We were made to enjoy him. The chief end of man is to glorify God and enjoy him forever. "Delight yourself in the Lord, and he will give you the desires of your heart." It seems a trick verse. At first, it sounds like the promise of some genie of the lamp, but look again. If you delight yourself in the Lord, then the Lord becomes the desire of your heart, and to grant that desire is simply to give us himself. Very clever. I may start out thinking of God as a way to get what I want, but in the end, he becomes all I want, and he is more than happy to grant our request for the thing that is most good for us, himself.

Ancient Roadmaps
To rejoice is to make one of the most powerful statements of faith possible in our broken world.

The Discipline of Rejoicing
Authentic joy is a statement of faith. Some traditions in the history of the church place a higher emphasis than others on joy. For some it is subsumed under worship, while others (like the Franciscans) bring a higher degree of intentionality to the command of scripture to rejoice. We

are told to "rejoice in the Lord always" (Phil 4:4), which is repeated for the slow of hearing, and to "rejoice when we fall into various trials" (James 1:2). Perhaps even more instructive is the command to "rejoice with those who rejoice and weep with those who weep" (Rom 12:15). What this verse does is remove naive notions that the injunction to rejoice means little more than "put on a happy face" or "don't worry; be happy." Nor does it permit us to legislate a smile over the true heart condition of our brother, or sister, or ourselves. It maps out an authentic engagement with God and others in the world. Joy is not denial. Joy is not a hollow, superficial laugh. Real joy is big enough to reverberate deep in the belly of the real world, and indeed to change this world. And so to rejoice is somehow to be truer to life, as it really is in Christ.

Our Lord did not model emotional aloofness but rather, incarnation. He took on humanity but also took humanity into himself, owning it all. He was true to the sorrows and joys of others because he made them his. Therefore because we are one body in Christ, the joy of others should be our joy, their sorrow our sorrow. The conditions of the body are shared by all members. "But God has combined the members of the body and has given greater honor to the parts that lacked it, so that there should be no division in the body, but that its parts should have equal concern for each other. If one part suffers, every part suffers with it; if one part is honored, every part rejoices with it" (1 Cor 12:26ff).

This degree of "owning" is beyond sympathizing. We don't sympathize with our hand when it is smashed in the door or envy our shoulders when they get a massage. We are one. We suffer and rejoice with all. This unity is impeded by the distance created by economic inequality. Our joy should be increased and multiplied by sharing, and our sorrows decreased and divided by the same process. But the distance created by wealth removes the rich from both the joys and the sorrows of the body of Christ. They may have only intended to remove themselves from shared sorrows, but they sever themselves from both. For followers of Christ detachment and stoicism are not really options.

With Christ as their model, the Franciscans knew that joy could only come by an authentic engagement with others in the body of Christ, by taking what others were going through into ourselves, allowing it to sink in because we know the joy of God is greater. They were not swallowed up in tragedy, but let the Hope of Christ redeem what could not be ignored. We are not speaking about erasure, but redemption. This is a real world. No "do over" is possible; great sorrow can only be removed by being transformed into greater joy. Consequently, real joy does not try to avoid the suffering in ourselves or others.

Practice: *"The kingdom of God is not meat and drink, but justice and peace, and joy in the Holy Ghost." (Rom 14:17). In obedience to the command to rejoice, and following the template of one of the Psalms, write a new Psalm of Joy. Then share the joy with someone after you have written and polished your Psalm.*

Questions: Poverty & Happiness

Guides
Joy of the Lord
What are some instances in your life that you can point to as examples of the joy of the Lord?

Companions
The Game of Life
Who is truly happy?

What assumptions do we have about the pursuit of happiness?

Are the best things in life really free?

True to Life
What does it mean to rejoice with those who rejoice and weep with those who weep?

What does the command to rejoice mean?

Journal
Fruit of Joy
What does joy look like in myself, in others?

Am I personally conflicted about joy?

When have I experienced the joy of the Lord as my strength?

Is there anything blocking my ability to receive the joy of the Lord, or to share in the sorrow and joy of others?

POVERTY & EXCLUSION

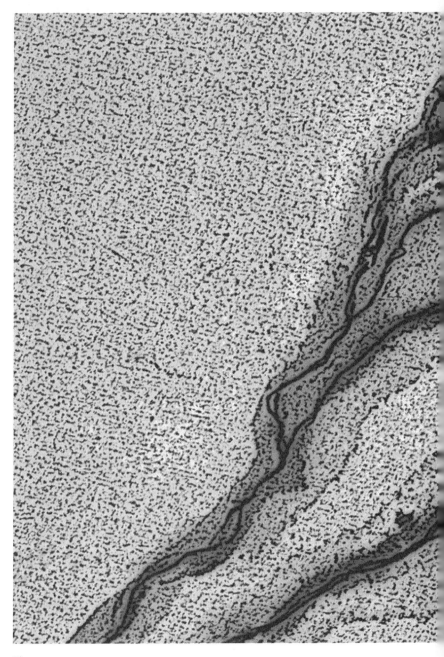

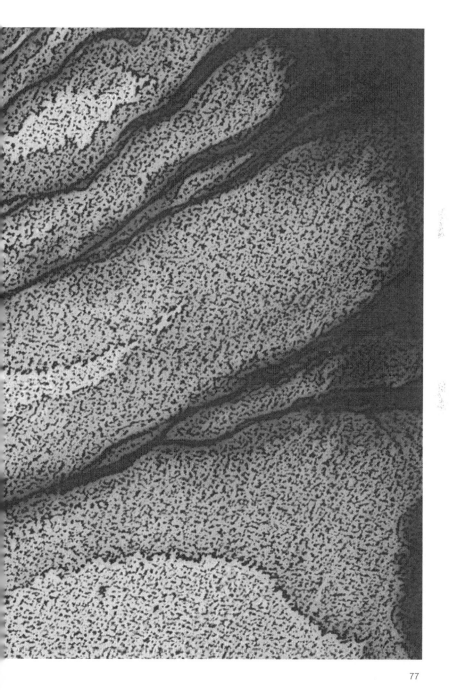

Taking a Bearing

One definition of injustice is doing only for a few, what we owe to each and everyone.

Imagine your life as a set of concentric spheres, each one extending out broader and further from the core (kind of like a perfectly round onion). At the core is the self, immediately ringed by your family, your close friends, followed by your community, your religious group, your church, your ethnic group, your gender group, your political party, your socioeconomic group, your national identity, your region, your generation, etc. Now imagine this onion represents your identity as ordered relationship structures in which the most important things, the things you most deeply identify with, are the deepest down.

The order can be different for each individual. For some, their ethnicity is a far more formative part of their identity than their nationality. For others, being part of a certain socio-economic group is more important than the local community in which they were raised. It tends to vary. Whatever the case, Christ directly challenges all of our identity relationships with his Kingdom model, by first asserting his place at the core, and by spelling out the radical consequences to all of our relationships when we put him in his rightful place. But isn't it a good thing to love our mothers, love our country, love ourselves? Indeed. Love is a good thing, but the real question is, "Why do the same people keep getting our love?" and "Why do others (whom God told us to love as we love ourselves) not even register on our radar?" We allow our little onion to define the limits of our love, because we are measuring out what we believe to be a finite resource, our capacity to love. Now imagine what happens when we extend the natural model out and universalize it. Everyone takes care of themselves and "their own" people first and eventually exclusively.

In times of (even perceived) crisis or scarcity of resources, the outer rings are ignored in order to provide first for the most important ones at the core. Anyone who is not in those inner circles becomes a competitor for those scarce resources, a threat to the things and people we hold dear. If it is a trade off between taking care of those with whom I identify or sharing with a broader group, I will always (most naturally) revert toward defense of me and mine. How could genocide happen in Rwanda? How could Germans embrace Naziism? How can Americans justify racism, wars, walls, camps, cages? Easy. Under the banner of fear and scarcity, it is either us or them, and "us" has become a much narrower identity. Lines are drawn ("you are either with us or against us"). The "natural" process of taking care of what we love becomes a defense of a much smaller identity group and a demonization of anyone falling outside our inner circle. It helps to think of "them" as less than human, criminals actively threatening our tiny enclave. This is how natural love becomes hate. Monstrous acts and injustice always seem to start as defense of family, tribe, and nation.[1]

The architects of the Holocaust that killed six million Jews were certainly following this concentric logic of relating to the world. Hannah Arendt was a journalist reporting on the Nazi bureaucrat, Adolf Eichmann's trial after the end of WWII. Beyond the evil of the architects, Arendt was even more appalled at how easily all of society and "unremarkable", "ordinary", "normal" people like Eichmann were able to participate in such heinous crimes against humanity. It wasn't that their loyalty to their own national and ethnic identity caused them to intentionally make one "final decision" to participate. Their involvement was far more insidious. The average citizen may not have been the primary architects of violence, but they did choose to go along with it and keep that evil system functioning in a thousand little bureaucratic decisions and mundane acts of complicity to genocide. For them, they were merely keeping the trains running on time, never mind they were headed to Auschwitz. She referred to this phenomenon as the "banality of evil."[2] She is not by any means belittling genocide, but rather showing us how participation in this evil was so ordinary that it did not even register as evil. Evil does not primarily reside in the masterminds of diabolical villains but in the hearts of every self-protecting citizen. Evil is executed, not just in the gas chambers but in tiny acts of preference and exclusion originating in board rooms and committee meetings, in civic organizations, in schools, and in churches.

We have spoken before of the apparent bias of God toward those who have the cards stacked against them in this life. We acknowledge and affirm that as a reflection of a deeper justice, even when we do not understand it. What identifying with that sort of God means for us, should be obvious. If we place Christ at the core of our life, then we can expect a radical and perhaps constant revision of our natural identity spheres, that moves us outward and them inward. We become biased like God toward the poor and excluded. It may well be that our capacity to give of our resources and time and attention is limited, and it may well be that we are already complicit in contributing in small ways to great evil. If that is the case, then justice in the context of the very real and brutal inequalities in our world, is not doing what comes naturally, but rather taking our love to the bottom first, to the outer rings, prioritizing those at the margins, first, those whom no one identifies as "our own".

---

[1] Volf, Miroslav Exclusion and Embrace: A Theological Exploration of Identity, Otherness and Reconciliation (Nashville: Abingdon Press, 1996), p. 210-215.

[2] Arendt, Hannah Eichmann in Jerusalem: a Report on the Banality of Evil (New York: Viking Press, 1963).

Charting a Course
Read Luke 14.

Jesus took the opportunity of a dinner party at the home of one of the chief Pharisees to reveal much about our natural biases. He couldn't even get in the door before he met with an opportunity to expose their self-righteousness. He healed (yet another) lame man on the Sabbath. They were all watching him to catch him out, and he pointed out how much more compassion they had for their livestock than people in their little worldview. Christ started watching them and noticed their desire to be honored, and in fact how something as seemingly generous as hosting a meal could hide their selfish intent.

The reason the righteousness of the Pharisees had nothing to do with real love was because it was based on reciprocity. That is how the world takes care of itself, I'll be good to those good to me, "love" those who benefit me. Christ disrupts this natural order by saying "When thou makest a dinner or a supper, call not thy friends, nor thy brethren, neither thy kinsmen, nor thy rich neighbours; lest they also bid thee again, and a recompense be made thee...When thou makest a feast, call the poor, the maimed, the lame, the blind: And thou shalt be blessed; for they cannot recompense thee." They must have sat around blinking in astonishment at the thinly veiled judgment. He then progressed into a parable of God hosting a meal and eventually inviting "the poor, and the maimed, and the halt, and the blind." This not only showed that God is not a respecter of persons (unlike the people in the room) but it revealed that God himself would likely be excluded from their VIP list of important persons, so much so, that they would probably make up every excuse not to attend his feast. The hardest saying of this encounter was reserved for a bigger crowd. To the multitudes that followed him he warned, "If any man come to me, and hate not his father, and mother, and wife, and children, and brethren, and sisters, yea, and his own life also, he cannot be my disciple." This is not an injunction to self-loathing or cruelty toward others. What Christ is saying here is a corrective on our natural inclinations. The reality is that we already take care of our own interests and those of our inner circle, quite naturally. We love our inner circle, our peeps; hatred is reserved for our enemies.

But Christ is not just tweaking the natural order; he is fulfilling it with love. What we are called to do (in contrast to what seems like the most natural good) appears like hating our own blood. You have heard the phrase "blood is thicker than water." It describes the way we relate to family, and the preference we give to them, not based on any merit, often overlooking faults, and some times doing what is downright unjust (or at least unfair) to their advantage. What mother doesn't take every advantage for her child's education? What brother would not come to the defense of a sibling, right or wrong? If you suddenly treated some stranger or enemy like a brother or a child of your own, wouldn't your own family see that as displacement of them and their privileges as family? Wouldn't that feel like downright hatred of mother and father and country? Sometimes obedience will even look like hating our own lives. What is more natural than to prioritize taking care of yourself over others when you have to make a choice with what little you have? The little boy who gave his own and his family's food to feed the five thousand is a good image of what Christian service feels like. There are so many, and we have so little. The instinct is to feed ourselves first.

We have pursued that sensible policy over the centuries, and it has only served to perpetuate greater disparity and injustice, as each prioritizes only their home, their church, their race, their narrow neighborhood. Natural good can disguise the self-serving seeds of oppression. Now Christ comes along, and suddenly even marginalized Samaritans are to be included in the definition of "neighbor", to be perceived as part of our community, not excluded from it, nor sacrificed to protect what is near and dear. Suddenly, there is no longer male and female, slave and free, Jew and Greek, but Christ is all and in all. There goes the neighborhood.

This very disruptive God is taking over all of the rings of the onion, not just the core. He is demanding the right to reshuffle our "inner circles" as he sees fit, to redefine who is whose brother's keeper, who is my neighbor, stretching the definition back to what it was before it shrank in the dryer of human sin. And if he calls us to go to a distant mission field to serve, that will definitely cost our family life and have an impact on our closest relationships. What if Christ says, "I want you to take these orphaned children on another continent into the inner core of your heart, in some way displacing the obligations you owe to your natural family"? Won't missing so many holidays be read as hatred of your kin?

What if Christ also says, "I know there are plenty of needs in your own country, but I'm asking you to give this man, who was displaced and now has no country, greater priority. Patriotism is all well and good, but I demand you take this refugee as your countryman in the Kingdom, as a fellow citizen of heaven." Won't that look like unpatriotic hatred of your earthly country? It will. And what if he went on to say, "That group of people whom you fear (and in some ways detest) because you believe they will take away what you think is yours, I want you to see them as your kinsman, as part of your community? The Muslims whom you have distanced yourself from for fear of civilizational war and terrorism, the

Chinese businessman whom you fear will take your place in the marketplace, the Latin immigrant whom you see as a drain on jobs and an unwelcome burden on your public health and education system, I want you to include them in your inner circle, to include them among those to whom you give preference. And Christians in poverty far from your shores, whom you fear might sap your every resource and that of your nation, I want you to give the same unfair benefits as your immediate family. They are your brothers and sisters." He is not just making a nice metaphor; family is a claim of relational priority. As Lord, Christ has every right to redefine all your priorities, reorder all your identities, remake all your loves.

Ancient Roadmaps
The choice is before us, a narrow existence, trusting in and rarely escaping the gravity of our selves, or a life of carrying and being carried by others. The latter way of inclusion and exchange is the lighter way to travel.

The Discipline of Exchange
The way of Christ is the way of substitutionary love. There is a long Christian tradition of understanding identification with others in love as a call to a life of substitutionary exchange. Its core scriptural imperative is Galatians 6:2 "Bear one another's burdens, and so fulfill the law of Christ." Strong in various Christian writings, from the desert fathers to Dante, the way of exchange experienced a brief revival of interest in the writings of Charles Williams and others in the 20th century. It is built on the premise that all life consists in relationships of exchange (God & man, man & man, man & creation, etc.) understood and lived at deeper and deeper levels.[3]

Level 1. Life is Inclusion. I am not all there is. We must admit (not resent) the existence of others. Other creatures have as much right to be and to will in this world as I. I may not like the will of others, but I must put up with (or better, accept) the fact of the existence of their wills. Accepting the existence of the unalterable Divine will, like it or not, is a part of being in relationship with reality. This first rudimentary kind of exchange makes space for "the other." Tolerance is a means of this exchange.

Level 2. Life is Interdependence. Mutuality is a fact; each depends on many others. Your life rests on the backs of generations who went before and countless others currently sustaining your life (and you, theirs) at this very moment. Society creates contracts to manage this exchange. This crafting of shared space (cooperation) is required to get things done and to sustain relationships. Partnership is one medium of this exchange.

---

[3] Williams, Charles, *Essential Writings in Spirituality and Theology* (London: Cowley,1993) and Williams, Charles, *The Figure of Beatrice: A Study in Dante* (Cambridge: D.S. Brewer, 2000). See also Merton, Thomas *No Man is an Island* (San Diego: Harcourt Brace & Co.,1983).

Level 3. Life is Love. The quality of life as exchange is enriched by living unselfishly. Each is to have sympathy with the other, to give continual attention to the needs of his loved ones, his neighbor, to work and to care for others beside himself. He whom "holy luck" throws in our way, into our space, is our neighbor. Acts of kindness are a medium of this exchange.

Level 4. Life is Union. The fourth level of exchange is union of existence in which we realize that love is not merely living *for* others; but living *in* others. By participating in the co-inherence of Christ we are members one of another, truly, spiritually, not just metaphorically. Love takes the lives of others into ourself, truly swapping spaces in the mystery of co-inherence. Substitution is a medium of this exchange.

The great substitutionary exchange that took place on Calvary was the ultimate measure of this kind of life and love. It exists in much smaller degrees in the person who finally can cease to worry about her burden because her friend has agreed to worry about, lose sleep, feel pain, pray over it on her behalf, *as if it were her own burden.* The love of substitutionary exchange is not to be taken lightly. Beyond seeking empathy or even praying for someone and their needs, it asks God to put you in the place of the other with all their needs and to be the instrument by which God bears their burden. When we bear each others' burdens we realize that what was heavy for me is lighter for you, and that God gives me the capacity to lift both you and your burden, though it is crushing you, as if it weighed nothing at all.

In the words of the Egyptian desert fathers, "It is right for a man to take up the burden for those who are akin to him, whatsoever it may be, and, so to speak, to put his own soul in the place of that of his neighbor, and to become, if it were possible, a double man; and he must suffer, and weep, and mourn with him, and finally the matter must be accounted by him as if he himself had put on the actual body of his neighbour, and as if he had acquired his countenance and soul, and he must suffer for him as he would for himself. For thus it is written, 'we are all one body'."[4]

Practice: *The discipline of exchange is a deep mystery of "in-othering", but mere attention to look for examples as well as opportunities to practice it ourselves, will develop our capacity beyond the lower levels towards co-inherence. Pair up with someone from this study group to discuss and practice at least the first three levels of the discipline of exchange for one week. Reflect how the discipline of exchange has altered who is in your inner circles.*

---

[4] *Saint Athanasius of Alexandria Collection* [five Books] (Aeterna Press, 2016), Bk I, Ch IX, 131. Like when Sam carried Frodo. Tolkien, J.R.R. *The Return of the King* (New York: Houghton Mifflin, 1955).

Questions: Poverty & Exclusion

Guides
Stretch
What are some changes God has made in your definition of "my neighbor" since going outside of your home context?

How has your experience of the global body of Christ revealed how we are members one with another?

Companions
Identify
What are some reasons we choose not to identify with those in suffering?

Can we think of instances where it was easier to give money to someone than to identify with them?

Onion Rings
What do our identity circles (our 'onion') look like, and what would radical redefinition by Christ do to that worldview? Draw what it looks like before and after Christ messes it up with love.

Space
What are ways we can create space in ourselves for others who are not in our inner circle, both going out to the margins and bringing in from the margins, those who very different from us?

Journal
Am I prepared to accept the consequences of letting God change my identity priorities, all the way to the core?

What does God's Word say about reconciliation and whom I should include?

How can I concretely enact inclusion for someone this week that can serve as a sign of the love God has shown when he brought me in?

Whose burden (besides my own) am I currently carrying? Is there something which God is asking me to carry?

Is there something he is asking me to give to him or to a member of his body to carry on my behalf?

POVERTY & POWERLESSNESS

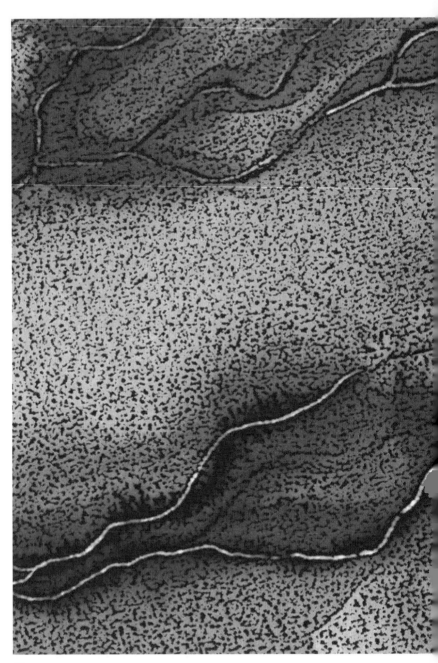

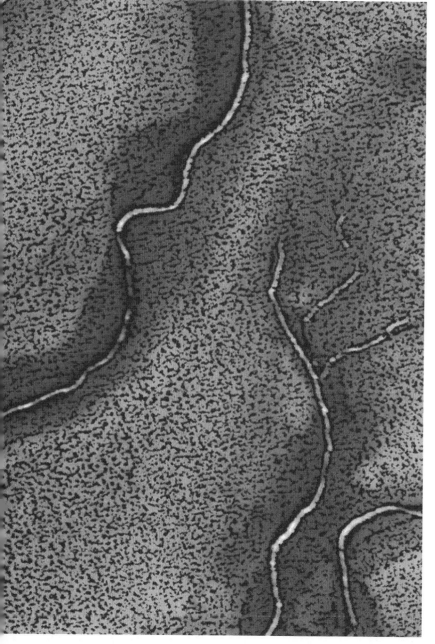

Taking a Bearing

Owning poverty is willingly embracing a condition of powerlessness.
The acknowledgment of our bankruptcy, our neediness is the essence of what it means to be poor in spirit. This posture of poverty (also known as humility), is a true picture of ourselves as dependents of the Creator God and supplicants of the merciful Savior God. It is absolutely necessary to honestly confront this true mirror of ourselves in this life. However, the responses to this truth can be very different, because it entails more than a mental assent of a label, it is a commitment to walk in the Way.

In particular, one aspect of poverty that is very difficult to willingly embrace is powerlessness. It is superficial to believe material poverty only effects material things. Physical lack diminishes not only opportunities but choices and even the power to choose, by degrees. Poverty is a loss of basic freedoms. This is why the poor are so often the victims of oppression and exploitation. Their own freedoms have long since been subjected to the will of others. They have traded subjection for survival. It is from this world of inexplicable powerlessness to our world of inexplicable personal power that we must turn to understand how far we are from owning poverty. To collect evidence that we have no sense or sympathy for what the powerlessness of poverty truly entails, we need only think about the last time not getting our way really set us off. We fume because some idiot took up our patch of road when we were trying to turn. We register a complaint when our order at the cafe is messed up or delayed. We are taught our whole consumer lives that it is our duty to complain for the greater good. We are also told more choice and more choices are an unquestioned good, which rests of course on the false assumption that our own will is good.

It is the law of entitlement. We love our privileges and rights (and often confuse the two), and we spend most of our time trying to award ourselves more power over our lives and the lives of others. When any of our rights appear to receive the slightest infringement, we go ballistic. We are so far removed from the willing abdication of our rights that our Master taught and modeled. When we suffer the loss of our property, we are told to give the exploiter more, the very shirt off our back. When we suffer the loss of our safety in physical violence, we are to offer that person another opportunity to punch us around again. When we are made to serve against our will, we are to over-deliver on the demands of our unjust oppressor...by going another mile (Matt 5:39ff).

That kind of willing abdication of our rights is so far out there from us. We still reel from the hurt to our dignity when we simply fail to get glowing affirmation from a parent, a boss, or teacher. Perhaps seeing the powerlessness of others first-hand will give us a sense of perspective, reduce to pettiness, our long list of tiny hurts, and make them easier to bear in comparison to the true life-and-death indignities some people have to suffer? Karl Barth describes such profound solidarity in poverty.

"The need of my fellow man, the need of his impotent attempt to live, the revelation of which makes him my neighbor, expresses itself like my own need in specific sicknesses, derangements and confusions of his psycho-physical existence. It expresses itself in the fact that his attempt to live is foredoomed to failure and confronted with death. I cannot really arrest this process either in its inner necessity or in its manifestations. I cannot help my neighbor to the extent that I can as little save him from death as I can myself. It is in the helplessness, with which we confront ourselves, that there consists the fellowship of sin and misery, into which I see myself placed by him and with him. And for that very reason I shall not speak to him of myself but of Jesus Christ: of Jesus Christ as the Helper who is the end of the process, of Jesus Christ who is life in death and beyond death. But how can I speak my word of witness, without substantiating it, making it my own word, by showing that I participate in the sicknesses, derangements and confusions of his psycho-physical existence: participate not only as a fellow-sufferer--the concept of sympathy is inadequate, as many in the world have more truly found than those in the Church--but as one who knows where help is to be found: Knows because I have already been actually helped in Jesus Christ in respect of my own sufferings. I can as little help my neighbor as myself. But I cannot be helped, as I am helped, without being laid under an obligation to tell my neighbor what help there might be...By my assistance I can only set up a sign of that assistance."[1]

Such empathic response to the powerlessness of my neighbor is a profound choice. For some, the tendency towards protection of their own rights becomes even stronger because an experience of poverty evokes in them a raw fear of powerlessness. Fear can drive a regressive self-control of our environment, as if we needed to step in as god to take care of a universe that is reeling out of control. We feel we need to take care of ourselves, since no one else will. To see poverty without seeing God's sovereign mercy through the eyes of faith, is a fearful vision. Who would willingly embrace vulnerability without trusting that a God of infinite love and power is in control, without having experienced first-hand, being rescued in our powerlessness? Here it is necessary to know experientially that "perfect love casts out fear."

---

[1] Barth, Karl *Church Dogmatics Volume 2* (New York: T&T Clark International, 2004), 444-5.

Charting a Course
Read Philippians 2:1-15.

This passage in Paul's letter to the Philippians is one powerful call to a spirit and posture of poverty. From the start we are told to be like-minded, like-hearted in love, and in fact to be so alike that we have one heart, for love and compassion. This fellowship of the Spirit manifests as esteeming others better than ourself, and looking beyond our own interests after the concerns of others. It is antithetical to the petty quarreling and honor-seeking that is our natural bent and which is rooted in a belief that we must hold onto our positions in order to protect our place in the pecking order.

It is the Holy Spirit who demands and enables a "climbing down" to a low position of great vulnerability, which Christ himself demonstrated. If you think you have interests that need protecting, or a high status in life you are afraid to lose, think of Christ, who, although God himself, laid aside the rights associated with that highest status. Because he deserved that status from all eternity, he felt no need to cling to it with a sense of entitlement. He had such matter-of-fact faith in his authority that he willingly changed his status, to that of the lowest man, a man with no rights, a slave. He more than embraced, he owned, the reputation and posture that went along with that form. As a slave is not his own property, Christ lived in obedience to the will of the Father, even though his will was co-equal with the Father's from all eternity. Just imagine how it would have felt for Christ to be constrained or bound. This is a puzzle. What kind of subjection is it when the will of Christ and the Father were (and are) identical? It is a profound mystery to say you submitted to the Father's will, when it is the same as your own.

There is something very powerful in the choice of Christ to submit to the will of the Father (as if it were an Other will). The necessity was not there in Christ to submit. Where there is unity, submission is not required for alignment of will. However, for us, there is no choice in our human condition apart from submission, subjection of our will to that Other's will. Is it clicking yet? The whole set up of Christ's incarnation, characterized by its limited revelation and knowledge, its "need-to-know" orders from the Father, was a true model of our impoverished condition. Oh, blessed Light, that Christ would not only save by grace but model the means of grace! For there are no other options for us. It is our will, the very core of our being, that is twisted. We cannot lift ourselves outside our own will...our wicked will isn't capable and wouldn't let us, if it were. Leave it to human pride to even find a way to believe we can become humble on our own. Absurd. Humility is willing the death of our will, choosing less choice, acting to surrender the very power to act. How exactly were you planning on doing that, without ending up with your same old will on the throne?

The only means by which we can escape the prison of ourselves is by no longer trusting that deceiver that is our own heart (who traps us as long as we trust in us) and by subjecting ourselves to the will of God. The fancy term for this is obedience. However, we cannot obey. And that is why (or one of the many reasons why) Christ, the second person of the Trinity both obeys on our behalf and is seen to obey. The subjection of his will (even though his will was already perfect) was showing us the only way out of slavery to sin and the prison of poverty's powerlessness, through obedience to God in Christ. It modeled the restoration of the natural order of things, the subjection of the created to the Creator, in the most amazing way, by the obedience of God the Son (Eternal, Uncreated) to God the Father. Think about the Will that spoke the universe into existence, whose very Word brought being from nothing, the Will against which there can be no contrary thought. His is the supreme Will that is ever obeyed. Imagine that Will voluntarily subjecting itself to obey the Father. If there was ever a case for someone exerting his rights, or being justified in his judgments, Jesus, eternal God from God, had that right to assert the supremacy of his Will. He did not. He took on humility instead. "Though he was rich, yet for your sakes he became poor, that through his poverty you might be rich" (2 Cor 8:9).

So much was happening on the cross. The redemptive work of God was driven by such perfect wisdom. Behold the obedience even unto death, the ultimate subjection of Christ's will (against all one's own better judgment, feelings, reason, and sight) to the Will of the Father. "Not my will but Thine be done", he said. Much flows from his model of voluntary obedience by logical necessity. First, faith is shown to be the true means of grace. See how it can be no other way? That poverty of unknowing shown to us by the Omniscient One presents obedience in faith as our only option. Our wills desperately want to know more, to control more outcomes, for ourselves. But we are corrupt judges passing corrupt verdicts on what we see and what we think we know.

Thank God, he did not leave us to our own devices but granted us Christ's obedience as model and substitute. In that image of the voluntary subjection of Christ's will he has shown us that the only way by which our wills can come out of self-bondage, is through slavery to God. The way out of spiritual poverty is through a spirit of poverty, the way out of death is through the death of our will. By subjection to God's will in Christ's obedience to the Will of the Father, we are made free. "it is God who works in you both to will and to do of his good pleasure." (Phil 2:13).

Everything in our corrupt nature revolts at those words. We would much rather define freedom as doing what we will. But if what we will always works to the ruin of ourselves and others; what kind of freedom is that? Our sinful will prevents our true freedom, our pride prevents our exaltation by God's hand. We must walk Christ's path of poverty by his Spirit to be lifted up like him. Herein we see we are not just "mostly poor", but totally impoverished. Even knowledge of God's way does not grant us the power to walk that path ourselves. We must call out for grace like a supplicant, who has no power at all, and knows it. His grace (gifted power) abounds as we recognize our poverty, our powerlessness to will any good, our sinfulness. "There should be nothing distressing in these thoughts about our poverty. To be nothing of oneself is the creaturely condition: and it is the very magnificence of the salvation offered us that makes it impossible for us to win it. When we realize that the void in us can be magnificently filled by God, then our poverty should delight us. But there *is* a distressing humiliation which makes our state lower than just that of creatures: we are sinners. We are not merely what is not, but what ought not to be."[2]

Touching our powerlessness brings us to a realization that things are both worse and better than we thought. It is not just the case that we are powerless to 'fix' the ills of the world; we *are* the ills of the world. We are as powerless as death. Suddenly, we see that the rescue of others and ourselves is utterly beyond us, but the unfathomably good news is that Christ came into the world precisely to save powerless sinners like us (1 Tim 1:15). So we cry out to the Savior who plumbed the powerless of death itself, whom the Spirit raised back to life, who alone conquered the powerlessness of death and became the resurrection and the life for us. We can try to remain distant from our powerlessness or we can run to it, embracing it as the void which announces God's sole power. "Man must accept his basic poverty and the omnipotence of God which can alone effect salvation. He must rejoice in both, and love them with the same love with which our Lord put himself into the hands of his Father, who alone could save him from death (Heb 5:7)."[3] The death and resurrection of Jesus Christ radically transforms our capacity to willingly own our own and others' powerlessness. "Although he was crucified through weakness, yet he liveth by the power of God. For we also are weak in him: but we shall live with him by the power of God towards you" (2 Cor 13:4). For those who have come to terms with (owned up to) this aspect of poverty, the cross of Jesus Christ becomes the very power of God, for those who believe.

---

2 Durwell, Francis Xavier, *In the Redeeming Christ* (1960), Christian Classics Edition (Ave Marie Press: Notre Dame, 2013),130.
3 *Ibid.*

Ancient Roadmaps

The metaphor of Christian discipleship as slavery loses its potency when we replace it with the more palatable words "servant" and "service".The ancient context restores the impact of the biblical call to slavery.

The Discipline of Submission

We as disciples are asked to submit. The apostles repeatedly refer to themselves as slaves and admonished others to be slaves of Christ. Christ himself said those who want to be great in the Kingdom must become the slave of all. The scripture presents the metaphor and language of slavery, assuming the audience is well acquainted with the institution and the metaphor's implications. In case the immediate negative associations with such an evil human institution are not clear, we would do well to recall what slavery meant in antiquity.[4]

1. Slaves were property. They were not their own persons. How does one come by such property? By capture in war or by purchase. The implication is that we were slaves already and our new Master, (not our self, nor any other master), has full right of possession and disposal of us.

2. Slaves were tools. They do not work for themselves. The implication is that our Master has right of use of us wherever, whenever, whatever.

3. Slaves had no status. They have no glory or authority of their own. Their fortunes are derivative and tied to the ups and downs of their Lord's fortunes. The implication is that everything we do is by the authority of our Master and for his honor.

4. Slaves had few personal rights. They are not entitled to property or fair treatment or protection from physical abuse. Complaints do not end service, just make one a bad slave. The implication is that our Master recognizes no claims of entitlement but gives and takes away freely.

5. Slaves had no family. Cattle are not free to make a separate home for themselves. The implication is that all are under our Master's household.

6. Slaves could be freed. Redemption is the commercial and legal term referring to the purchasing of a slave's freedom. The implication is that our emancipation depends on our new Master.

---

[4] For a thorough source book on ancient slavery including its use in early Christian metaphor, see Wiedemann, Thomas, *Greek and Roman Slavery* (London: Routledge, 1981).

"What? Know you not that your body is the temple of the Holy Ghost which is in you, which you have of God, and you are not your own? For you are bought with a price: therefore glorify God in your body, and in your spirit, which are God's" (1 Cor 6:19).

"You were sealed with that Holy Spirit of promise which is the down payment of our inheritance until the redemption of the purchased possession, unto the praise of his glory" (Eph 1:14).

"Forasmuch as you know that you were not redeemed with corruptible things, as silver and gold, from your vain behavior received by tradition from your fathers, but with the precious blood of Christ, as of a lamb without blemish and without spot" (1 Pet 1:18).

The call to voluntary submission in the unambiguous language of slavery, is very hard, especially for those who have experienced abuse of power in their lives. It is clear that this word for the oppressed is emancipation from their slavery, through Christ. But those who have known power are called under Christ's yoke as slaves to practice powerlessness (Matt 11:29).

Practice: You can get a small taste of the discipline of slave-like submission by voluntarily subjecting your will for 24 hours to a trusted person in the role of master. This does not mean only responding in obedience to whatever they want you to do, but rather, not doing anything of your own will. It is also not enough to merely ask for permission for what you want. If you are a slave, then the goal is not doing, not wanting, anything unless specifically requested by your master, anticipating what they want, waiting on them. This discipline is not for the faint of heart. But as a healthy counter-weight to our normal spirit of entitlement, voluntary submission can provide a unique encounter with the powerlessness of poverty, and restore the posture of obedience behind the title we lightly throw around, "Why do you call me 'Lord, Lord' but not do what I say?" (Luke 6:46).

Questions: Poverty & Powerlessness

Guides
Two Responses
Give an example of a time when in response to an infringement of your rights you: 1. reacted to defend your honor and to uphold "the principle of the thing" and 2. reacted by taking your self lightly.

How have the thousand tiny humiliations of cross-cultural living helped or hindered your living by Philippians 2?

How has the poverty you have seen effected your capacity to embrace powerlessness?

Companions
Powerlessness
What are some examples of powerlessness, lack of opportunities and choice, or even the will to choose, that we have observed?

How does observing powerlessness in others make us feel?

How do we make sure what we experience of poverty has a positive impact (ie. that we do not regress in fear of powerlessness)?

Can we identify instances where we were able to see beyond visible powerlessness to see God's power at work?

Slaves
Now that we know more about it, do we think the metaphor of discipleship as slavery is still relevant today?

How can we emphasize the liberation *from* poverty for those who are already oppressed and the liberation *of* poverty for those with privilege?

Journal
Do not be Afraid
What fears block my willingness to trust God's Will, to relinquish the role of myself as god, and to obey? Whose will do I really trust?

How does the model of Christ's humility help me relinquish my rights?

POVERTY & HUNGER

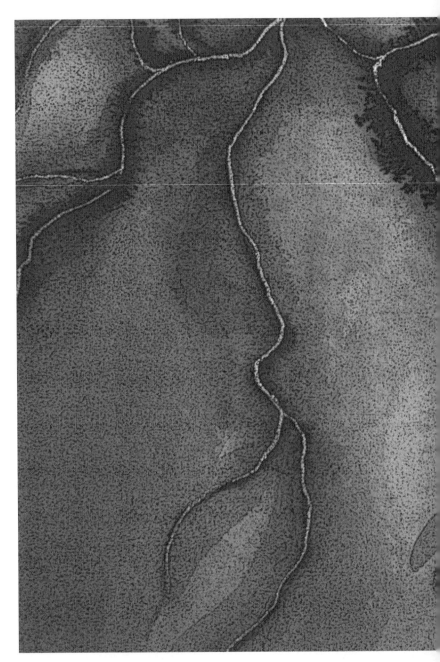

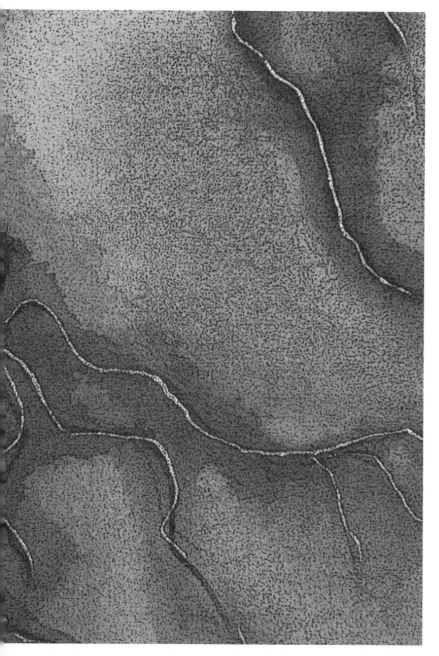

Taking a Bearing
Hunger is the visceral experience of poverty.

We have been describing the truth of spiritual and physical poverty as a condition, and moving toward greater acknowledgment of (and identity with) this condition. However, it is important to note that the engagement with this truth requires far more than a mental assent to poverty as a fact. Francis of Sales writes, "'To recognize one's wretchedness is not humility. It is merely not being stupid.' Spiritual authors never tire of telling us this: humility is a combination of a true realization of ourselves in God's sight and a love of that truth—to be wholly poor in the face of God's holiness, to recognize and love that poverty, in order that God may be wholly in us. Knowledge is not enough."[1] In fact, it is the experience of this reality that make it so difficult to 'own'. We could all come to a place where we mouth the words or conceptualize the fact that at the core of our experience of life is poverty, the brokenness of evil and sin. This gap (between what is and what should be) characterizes our relationships with each other, with the whole created order, and with the God who made us. Our inability to do anything about it ourselves is (according to the Bible) the spiritual equivalent of being dead in our trespasses and sins, death being the ultimate image of human poverty.

While our brokenness is a fact that the work of Christ remedied, the experience of the condition is something rarely addressed. We avoid this conversation to our peril, because much of our bondage and blindness and idolatries stem from a root avoidance of the experience of the poverty of the human condition. In addition, many Christians fail to come to terms with the paradox of the persistence of this experience after they have received saving grace. There are a thousand tricks of mind and theologies devised to wish away an ongoing experience of the pain of poverty, which is in fact, the Way of the Cross.

So, what is the experience of our condition like? Hunger. If we knew nothing other than the alienation and exploitation of the world and our own hearts, we probably wouldn't feel like fish out of water and long for what isn't there. It is the mixture of beauty and brokenness that brings deep sorrow. God has put eternity in our hearts, and so everything short of right and full relationship (union) with God and his creation is an aching hole at the core of our being. Hunger. We feel it in the experience of a world in which humans are dehumanized, objectified, abused, and exploited as tools, their value reduced to what market forces dictate or reduced to slaveries of a more degrading kind in the sex trade. While

---

[1] Durwell, Francis Xavier, *In the Redeeming Christ* (1960), Christian Classics Edition (Ave Marie Press: Notre Dame, 2013), 128, quoting St. Francis of Sales, *Les Vrais Entretiens Spirituels*, VI, p.404.

others still are ruthlessly eliminated in a context of competitive value, at the hands of oligarchs, warring ethnic groups, or even their own parents to preserve a lifestyle. Our objectification of animals in industrialized agriculture and the mass destruction of oceans and forests for profit are parallel examples of our destroying the inherent dignity and diversity of God's creation.[2] It is not right, and we long for it to be made right. Hunger.

Our inward journeys are often just as overwhelming. The brokenness we see in macro in the structural evils of this world find their origins in micro in our own hearts (James 4:1). That interior landscape is equally war-torn. And it is not just the aftermath of sin, but its continued action in our lives that make our heart our least favorite country to visit. It takes a lot of repression to live under the delusion one is doing fine in a Christian works model. To do so, one needs to emphasize a certain shortlist of sins and reduce them to external behaviors (do this, don't do that), so that merit is manageable, then spend a lot of energy judging and condemning notable public expressions of the condition in others to create a false sense that we are different and do not share the common poverty of humanity. In fact, it is a revived neo-Pharisaism. In Galatians, Paul asks the church who deceived them, "that having started by the Spirit they now should finish by human effort?" (Gal 3:3). It is a very good question that bears repeating today. If you want to live by that false system, it will require you to constantly run away from that aching hunger within that points to poverty. It is an exhausting, endless treadmill running from the fear that you are not (or won't continue to be) accepted by God on the basis of grace.

The works model also advises us to especially disguise any manifestations of poverty in public. Avoid any tradition that resembles public or interpersonal confession. If you must do counseling, gravitate toward counsellors who won't probe too much. Avoiding poverty because of the shame and hunger of it, is a sure way to avoid healing and transformation. In the same way, the unbeliever avoids salvation because of the scandal of grace. A gift can be received no other way than empty handed. Acknowledging my bankruptcy is prerequisite to receiving God's donation. "If we say we have no sin, we deceive ourselves and the truth is not in us, but if we confess our sins, he is faithful and just to forgive us our sins and to cleanse us from all unrighteousness" (1 John 1:8ff).

We cannot trick God into awarding us value according to our standards. It is doubly painful to receive the merit of Another by substitution. No one enjoys the feeling of being a charity case beggar with nothing but poverty

---

[2] Encyclical Letter *LAUDATO SI'* of the Holy Father Francis on Care for our Common Home (May, 2015). http://w2.vatican.va/content/dam/francesco/pdf/encyclicals/documents/papa-francesco_20150524_enciclica_laudato-si_en.pdf

to contribute, but if that is the truth, then we had better feel it. Yes, you say, but aren't Christians beyond that experience after saving grace? Going to that hard place of experiencing hunger, is itself an act of receiving grace from the God who fills us. He continually calls us there. While the world spends all its energies denying, reducing, or escaping from the experience of this reality, we not only go there, but find there life and health and peace. Christian discipleship is not a life of artificial denial but is characterized by heightened internal and external awareness of our true poverty and consequently...hunger.

Charting a Course
Read Matthew 5:1-5.

The discomfort and ambiguity of the gap (between what is and what should be) creates a more (not less) poignant hunger in the Christian life. That experience of the powerlessness over sin in our hearts and evil in the world should drive us, like Paul to lament the fact before God and seek his grace in our poverty (Rom 7). The wonder of grace that alone out-spans our poverty and abounds beyond the scale of our sin, is sufficient. God's strength is made perfect in our weakness.

Unfortunately, many respond in just the opposite way, denying that empty feeling of hunger, even denying that we Christians still sin (a lot!). They construct a Christian behavioral merit system to deny the ongoing spiritual bankruptcy of the self. Somehow many Christians get the idea that once they are saved, they get a blank slate and a ticket to heaven, but then it is all up to them to earn value from God in their life. Nothing could be further from the truth. God owns our poverty and development, and "I am confident that he who began a good work in you will carry it on to completion until the day of Christ Jesus" (Phil 1:6).

This grace model points us toward embracing our condition of poverty, and that means embracing hunger, the experience of poverty, as well. Christ was revealing something of this mystery when he said, "Blessed are those who hunger and thirst after righteousness, for they shall be filled." (Matt 5:6). His converse statement was, "those who are well have no need of a physician" (Mark 2:17). He is basically saying we can choose to deny or disguise our true illness of poverty and miss out on true healing and filling, but that if we are willing to go there, he will meet us at our deepest point of need.

It is a twisted logic that refuses help because we cannot bring ourselves to admit we are desperately needy. Beyond admission, it is even harder to *be what we are*, in all of its discomfort. To sit there in our poverty, silence the excuses, simplistic answers, distractions, and false comforts and just feel our hunger in the presence of God, is one of the hardest aspects of our relationship in Christ. Comfort may not come, but if true comfort does come, it will only come through the Holy Spirit our Comforter.

C. S. Lewis took the Cupid and Psyche myth and retold it in *Till We Have Faces*. In the original myth the lover loses the relationship with the god who has wed her because she breaks the rule of faith and takes a candle in to reveal the god in their bed chamber. Thanks to the influence of doubt introduced by her sister, she begins to imagine he is a monster. The god awakes; the fragile trust is broken. She is banished and must complete a series of impossible tasks in an amazing journey before she is restored. She experiences grace even in her tasks, and she as well as her sister are finally redeemed. Lewis uses the myth to describe the soul on a quest for the truth in the context of our broken relationship with God. At the beginning the protagonist in complaint asks, "Why must holy places be dark places?" Why is it that the more we seek that place of relationship with God, the light recedes? Many Christian mystics have articulated that the dark night of the soul is what the experience of true relationship with God feels like, both because it reflects our true condition and because in true relationship we no longer seek benefits or comforts, but God himself.

In the end the woman in the myth discovers that she cannot experience truth until she is real. By way of reply to her own first question she asks, "How can the gods meet us face to face till we have faces?"[3] It may be that the reason we do not experience more of the reality we seek is because we are not being real. An encounter and relationship requires two parties, but what if one of the parties can't help but play charades? There won't be much of a true exchange. To see a glimpse of one's self in its true condition may be a prerequisite to deeper relationship in the exchange of grace. It is not only a right posture then, it is a condition of authenticity, which is required. The former must spring from the latter in order to be genuine. We can mime humility. If I am not myself in my true state, what exactly am I pretending to bring to God? He only saves sinners. If what I bring is not I, as I am, then I am trying to encounter the Other with something that is not me. And then we wonder why he seems distant and cannot be found; it might be we who have failed to honestly turn up for the meeting.

"The poor in spirit who acknowledge themselves to be sinners, they do not need to know the least thing about the difficulties which appear when

---

[3] Lewis, C.S. *Till We Have Faces: A Myth Retold* (New York: Harcourt, Brace,1957). See also Cavanaugh, William T, *Being Consumed: Economics and Christian Desire* (Cambridge: Eerdmans, 2008).

one is neither simple nor humble-minded. But when this humble consciousness of one's self, i.e., the individual's being a sinner, is lacking —aye, even though one possessed all human ingenuity and wisdom and had all accomplishments possible to man, it will profit him little. Christianity will in the same degree rise terrifyingly before him and transform itself into absurdity or terror, until he learns, either to renounce it, or else, by the help of what is nothing less than scientific propaedeutics, apologetics, etc., that is, through the torments of a contrite heart, to enter into Christianity by the narrow path, through the consciousness of sin."[4]

Ancient Roadmaps
It is normal and necessary for Christian health to both admit and embrace in Christ the spiritual hunger at the root of human spiritual poverty.

The Discipline of Confession

Christ told us "blessed are those who hunger and thirst after righteousness, for they shall be filled." (Matt 5:6). Unfortunately we as individuals and as societies hunger after so many other things instead. We try to pretend it is not so, but honesty about our personal and corporate hungers must lead us to confession. And what do we confess? Hungers for the wrong things, insufficient hunger for the right things. We not only confess the private sins of our own personal thoughts, and words and deeds, but those of our communities. Culpability can be disguised or spread across a society or divided up into silos, but to own poverty is to admit that the sins of our church, the sins of our neighborhood, the sins of our society, the sins of our privileged group, are indeed ours. How will we ever come to hunger sufficiently for what is good, if no one owns up to their other hungers?

Consequently, self and corporate confession is vital to the spiritual journey, especially that awareness of what we are hungering for. "The heart is deceitfully wicked above all else, and desperately wicked: who can know it?" (Jer 17:9). Thanks to our hearts, we are right now, as close to the truth, to God, as we want to be. It is also our heart's habit of chasing artificial comforts along the way that causes us to break off our pursuit of God (or rather flee his pursuit of us). We are simply not sincere about our hunger. C. S. Lewis once claimed that if we were able to thoroughly pursue what we hunger for, in what he called an honest "dialectic of desire", that doesn't lie to itself when it is not truly satisfied but keeps hunting for what does satisfy, we would all find our way to God

---

4 Kierkegaard, Soren, "The Preparation for a Christian Life" in *Selections from the Writings of Kierkegaard*, Trans Lee M. Hollander (New York: Doubleday Anchor, 1960), 217.

eventually. The trouble is, we settle for cheap substitutes. George Herbert similarly spoke of a "repining restlessness" which is a gift of God designed to keep us ultimately unsatisfied with anything less than God.

When God at first made man,
Having a glasse of blessings standing by,
'Let us', said He, 'poure on him all we can;
Let the world's riches, which dispersed lie,
Contract into a span

So strength first made a way;
Then beautie flow'd, then wisdome, honour, pleasure;
When almost all was out, God made a stay,
Perceiving that, alone of all His treasure,
"Rest" in the bottom lay.

'For if I should,' said He,
'Bestow this jewell also on My creature,
He would adore My gifts in stead of Me,
And rest in Nature, not the God of Nature:
So both should losers be.

'Yet let him keep the rest,
But keep them with repining restlessness;
Let him be rich and wearie, that at least,
If goodnesse leade him not, yet wearinesse
May tosse him to My breast.'[5]

Our hunger may end up being our best ally and truest companion on the Godward journey, because it can clarify the Good we seek. Guigo, Prior of Charterhouse, in the dialogue of his *Meditations* explains that if it weren't for the suffering of our soul, we would fail to seek, miss out on, the true Healer, and be deceived by false remedies.

"O, man who have your sorrow, do you wish to ease it?"
"I do."
"For time or for eternity?"
"For eternity."
"Desire, then, eternal easement, that is the truth, God. For that is why he has struck you, that you might desire him, not herbs, not bandages."[6]

---

[5] Herbert, George "The Pulley" in *The Works of George Herbert in Prose and Verse Vol II* (London: William Pickering, 1846). See also Piper, John, *Desiring God: Meditations of a Christian Hedonist* (Multnomah, 1987). Tozer, A. W. *The Pursuit of God* (Harrisburg: Christian Publications, 1948).
[6] *Meditations of Guigo, Prior of the Charterhouse*. Trans John J. John (Wisconsin: Marquette UP, 1976).

Guigo prescribes a life of brutally honest (but matter-of-fact) spiritual dialogue and confession that employs repentance as a tool for relational knowledge of God. It is not so much knowledge about God that we need or crave. Having God as a concept in our head does not bring us nearer to his person. The discipline of confession reveals another way. The impediment to our filling our ultimate hunger, our union with God is none other than ourselves. Guigo painstakingly identifies the lusts, the false hungers, that attempt to quench our deepest hunger with false remedies, focusing on creatures rather than the Creator. Temptation is the proposal of an alternative good that will not meet our deepest need. Heresies are comforts or satiations promised by other "gods" or idols. Meanwhile, we have no idea how weak and sinful we really are, since we desperately try to preserve some scrap of our false self image of good. For example, our craving after spiritual experiences in themselves, instead of the God behind them all, is also a falsity. In this as in other sins, we accept a false comfort instead of the Comforter. We actually need hunger to propel us onward. The closer we get to God the closer we approach the honest state of our deprivation of soul, feel its poverty, and find God alone able to heal it. One consolation Guigo offers then, is the fact that even our infidelities can teach us about God's faithfulness. All of our confessed sins are forgiven, and they also remind us what the true God is not like.

Pascal asks "What else does this craving, and this helplessness, proclaim but that there was once in man a true happiness, of which all that now remains is the empty print and trace? This he tries in vain to fill with everything around him, seeking in things that are not there the help he cannot find in those that are, though none can help, since this infinite abyss can be filled only with an infinite and immutable object; in other words by God himself."[7] If we all have this God-shaped vacuum, we would do well to look earnestly at that empty space. For in our hunger we have the outline of the God who can fill us.

Practice: One way to identify our idolatries, our false hungers and comforts, is the dialogue modeled by Guigo. Start by naming something you desire and explaining why you want it. Then ask why you think you hunger for that? Proceed from there to repeatedly ask "why?" again of your own explanations at least three more times. Employ this tool of self-revelation to allow the Spirit to identify what requires confession and repentance, asking God to return your heart from these other inferior desires to pursue him alone to fulfill your deepest hungers.

---

[7] From *Pensées* 148, quoted in Morris, Thomas V. *Making Sense of it All: Pascal and the Meaning of Life* (Grand Rapids: Eerdmans, 2002), 134.

Questions: Poverty & Hunger

Guides

Self Awareness

What role has honest ownership of your own poverty in hunger played in your journey?

Companions

Macro & Micro

What have we experienced of injustice and evil in the world that sheds light on something we didn't like in our own hearts?

What have we learned about our own spiritual poverty that has shed light on social evil we have observed in the world?

Why is grace is so difficult to embrace?

Journal

Be Real

What ways have I attempted to avoid the experience of my own poverty?

Receive Grace

Do I believe God delights in me and offers me his favor today, even in my spiritual poverty?

How prepared am I to go there, to the hard places of self awareness?

POVERTY & INJUSTICE

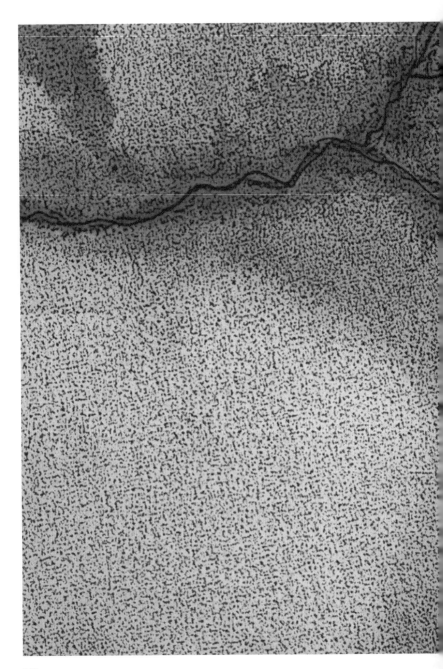

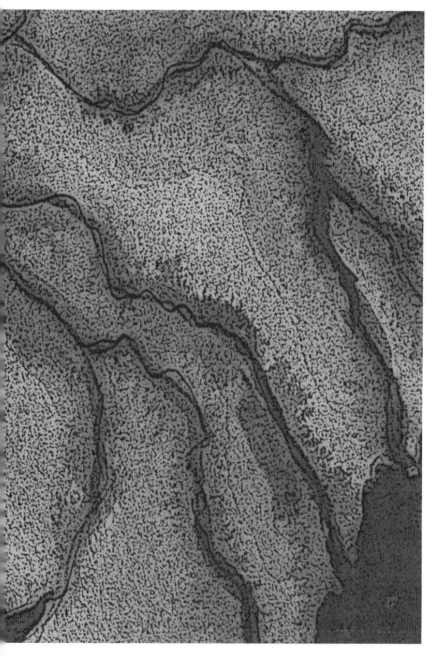

Taking a Bearing
What is, *will not tell us* ***what ought to be.***

One very common but dangerous mode of thought today starts out to explain poverty but ends up very subtly justifying poverty as a natural phenomenon. I have heard (otherwise sane) Christians explain that when Christ says "the poor you always have with you" (Matt 26:11), it is arguing against doing anything to end or alleviate poverty for others because the passage clearly describes its inevitability. There is a lot going on in that misguided interpretation. But the key error of thought seems to be deriving our ethical response from the descriptive or even prophetic conditions of the world. It would be equally culpable to interpret the passage, "because iniquity will abound, the love of many will wax cold" (Matt 24:12), as an injunction to give up on love and cease resisting sin. Christ's extensive teachings about our love obligations to "the least of these" are pretty obvious indicators that the existence of the poor, even the recurring tendency of inequality, should inspire solidarity and service with the poor, not negligence or passive assent toward injustice.

The values that define what is good are not derived from the way things happen to be at any given moment. I can see that some creatures in the animal kingdom eat their young; that is an observed fact. What I do with that fact ethically is not itself determined by the fact. Shall I set up that fact as a model for human behavior, or as despicable? Just because something exists, does not tell one whether there should be more or less of it. *What is* fails to determine *what ought to be.* Also, to remove the ideal removes motivation for change. No motion away from injustices like slavery, human trafficking, labor exploitation, oppression of women, racial inequality, have ever been possible under the assumption that the *status quo* is already good enough, or that the 'natural' is the place to look for the model of the good. One cannot derive a transformational ethical response to poverty (or anything), from mere human observation.

That seems really obvious, but it is important to realize that without a guiding notion of what is good, beautiful, and true, that is grounded in the biblical vision of God's will for humanity, we cease to speak intelligently about poverty and injustice. Christians are called to actively select for the good and reject what is evil. If we look at inequalities and disparity as just the way things work, (some get rich, some get poor) without any reference to the good of God's will, as imaged in God's Kingdom, we will end up in the same mode of justifying whatever is and trying to call it good. For example, Christian justifications of unchecked, market-governed growth as the best economic model, derive from this overly passive way of thinking about the good. "Things just grow unequally, so we should allow nature and the market to take its course. Eventually all the benefits of that unequal growth will trickle down to all. If things tend toward disparity, then it is better to have a big unequal pie divided up than a small unequal one. So the right thing to do is remove any checks on growth, and let market competition sort out the good for us."

Let's be clear; the premise is spot on; things do grow unequally. This is true in nearly every sphere of life. If left unchecked, things multiply from small beginnings. In the natural world, some things grow better in certain places than others. There are some plants that are so hardy they can dominate an area and completely choke out the life of other plants. In the animal kingdom, some animals are predators and others end up running their whole lives. In the economic sphere there are also strong and weak players. Unfortunately, modern notions of justice often only extend to discussions about equal opportunity, as if a fair race only consisted in starting the race at the same time from the same starting blocks. We struggle to effectively take the moral consequences of inequality into account, namely, that in our "fair" foot race, one fellow has one leg, another has no legs.

People tend to get upset when their economics are described as unjust, so the focus moves away from the issues of disadvantage and privilege to discussions about good rules to prevent cheating. But even if everyone plays by the rules, there is still deep injustice generated from inequality. Imagine the inequalities evident starting a Monopoly game half way through. Even when all the players follow the rules, there is very slim chance the new contestant would be anything other than a frightened renter until their money ran out, and they were bankrupt. But American culture loves the rags-to-riches story and amplifies the very rare exceptions that justify a hands-off economic posture, which essentially preserves and compounds inequality.

Not only are there inherent inequalities in individual and community capacity and resources, but inequalities are compounded generationally. Privilege and power can be accumulated and passed down in families and other institutions, further shaping the environment in which competition takes place. Because of these deep inequalities there are some who (on their own) will simply never get out of poverty in their lifetime, and "the poor you will always have with you." That still doesn't tell us what we should do about it. Our moral conclusion does not derive from the fact. If I say, "the stronger typically wins in a fight", it is not the same thing as saying, "the strong *should* win" or "might makes right." That is to take the inequalities of the world as given and allow the world to define the good on its own dog-eat-dog terms. That is what we actually do when we operate as if economic growth itself were *the good*.

The good describes what should be in relationships, compared to the way things are, and evokes an intervention of justice. In the case of this created order, the only just judgment and intervention comes from outside it, from its Creator. In God's good design, one quickly recognizes that in order for growth to continue to be and do good, it must have boundaries. Unchecked growth quickly ceases to be a good, not only for those threatened by it, but even for the one growing. In the body the unchecked growth of cells is cancer; in a garden, unchecked growth is weeds. In economics it is monopoly, in leadership, corruption, in society, lawlessness, in agriculture, monoculture, in personal morality, trespass. In our day of extreme individualism, it is very unpopular to speak of the benefits of government, but unchecked growth in the realm of personal freedoms and consumption has created an unbounded environment that is neither good for the individual exercising their right to unbounded wants, nor for those who have to live in a world with so many other individuals refusing to take "no" for an answer. The old adage that one's own lifestyle choices "aren't hurting anybody" is simply untrue.

So we must craft an ethical response in light of two facts, 1. the equality of inherent worth, in light of our creation in the image of God (which spells out that I am not of more worth than my neighbor nor more deserving of the privilege of flourishing in life), and 2. the inequality generated and perpetuated by differences in capacity and environment as well as systems that preserve and direct wealth and power. If things do grow unequally, the ethical response requires equalizing intervention, compensation. An absence of intervention is allowing the strong (and strength itself) to determine the good. It follows that we are morally obliged to select for weaker things, and in fact use ourselves as a human counterweight against the onslaughts of the strong (Proverbs 24:11). Our weighing in on behalf of the most vulnerable, the little ones, is not some random bias, but a logical consequence of seeking justice for all, in a context where things have grown imbalanced.

If the world were a vacuum and just starting out, a Christian could conceive of doing justice by measured, balanced means. But in a context in which the strong already prevail over, exploit, neglect, and consume the weak, there is only one side of the scales we can be on and still be just. To do justice today amidst grave injustice is to compensate for those cultures, communities, and individuals whose own growth has been squelched or overshadowed by the dominant individuals, institutions, and monocultures of our day. We can no longer blindly affirm that economic growth is the good, and we acknowledge that limits are both necessary and part of the definition of God's good for all humans to flourish. We are left with the question, what limits, what checks, make for life in all its fullness, especially for those who are the least of these?

Charting a Course
Read Romans 8.

From the earliest descriptions of God's created ideal for humanity and all subsequent Divine interventions for our good, we learn about the quality of justice which God intends for human flourishing. We are told that God set Man and Woman as stewards over all creation, and then put them in a garden to tend it. Eden provides particularly useful language to speak about justice. If left untended, a garden is quickly overgrown. Gardening as a process requires vigilant care for the soil and pretty consistent weeding. As an organic metaphor for justice, gardening affords powerful concepts like hoeing and pruning. The image of the good gardener is one who selects and deselects intentionally, not arbitrarily. The garden creates an environment that protects the weaker plants, and thereby intentionally selects for greater diversity. It is that active shaping of space, for the weaker things to live along side the strong, that gives us our best image of justice as a descriptor of a principle shaping relationships on the Divine pattern, rooted in love. It is a wonder of God's generosity that we were created to assist in this just effoliation of his creation.[1]

But what if those set up as stewards over this creation were themselves unchecked? If they were just governed by what they felt like and wanted, would they not be unjust in their management? Very quickly their domain would be more like "Lord of the Flies" than Eden. It is very clear that the governors need to be governed. Many Christians emphasize the human right of dominion over creation without emphasis on the derivative responsibility entailed in the role. No matter how much power we claim and exercise over others and the world, without our own submission under God's government, without a check on our own growth and consumption, we forfeit our true God-given role as sub-agents of justice.

It is deeply significant that the original boundary that God provides for human stewardship is a self-check, in the form of a limit on consumption. "You can eat anything you want...but not this one thing, the fruit of the tree of the knowledge of good and evil." This is a valuable reminder in an era in which the consequences of unchecked human consumption and exploitation of the natural world (and each other) are spiraling out of

---

[1] Tolkien, J.R.R. *Tree and Leaf* (London: HarperCollins, 2001).

control. Ever since original sin, leaving humans to our own devices has brought the worst "natural" consequences, as the earth and the weaker children of men are literally consumed by the strong.

In the Fall, we were unable to self-govern our own appetites and wills; we wanted to be like gods, unchecked in our own power to decide what we want and what we will have. As a consequence of our inability to self-regulate, God introduced an extreme external check on humanity, death. In Romans 8:20 Paul describes it as being subject to futility. We were subjected to the same forces of violent competition for survival and corruption that shape the lives of plants, animals, and microbes.

Death certainly sets a finite limit to the unchecked appetites of humanity, which has repeatedly demonstrated that its members will consume anything and anyone in their way. We begin to understand death as a gracious limit on our capacity to imagine and execute evil. Now at least we have a limited time within which to grow our wills, bent on self-aggrandizement. Then comes death, the great leveler. Unfortunately, one can still do a lot of damage even in those short seventy years. One can cause irreparable harm to one's self, the world and others, especially if we were to get organized. Human empire dodges the limitations on brutality.

God's gracious intervention to destroy and scatter Babel gives humanity the benefits of decentralization and diversity, without which, the weak have very little space or voice. With no distance, people have no place to hide, and the forces of centralized human tyranny will eventually exercise control over all of their lives. The distance of a different culture and language, the remoteness of a mountain, an island, are a further chance for humanity to flourish and diversify. It is a wonder and grace of God's intervening justice that some small cultures have found a way to survive into the 21st century through remoteness.

In the last days, we are told that a government counter to Christ will exercise complete control over what people buy, sell, and trade across the whole world. Until very recently, such a degree of control over humanity was not conceivable. But now with the erosion of languages, the reach of technology, and the dominance of a monolithic culture of globalization, economics has the potential to be the means of a new universal quasi-voluntary enslavement. To see the repeated historical patterns of exploitation goes a long way toward explaining why humanity would need such a radical Divine external check on Babel, on our habit of consolidating power. It was a severe pruning of human injustice run amok. As with God's earlier just intervention in the Flood, injustice had once again become the norm with Babel, and the scales needed to be reset.

With the selection of Abraham and the people of Israel, the story of justice takes a familial line. God separates a people for himself, to and by whom he will speak about justice as his intent for humanity, and through whom he will bless all people. They received circumcision as a sign of those whom God has marked with a radical departure from natural, unchecked appetites. Circumcision is a (somewhat literal) sign of checked sexual appetite. In their Divinely designed cultural life, limits were applied to this family's consumption. Food restrictions were further signs of the sanctification of those living under God's just checks and balances.

In the law of the Lord given through Moses, we have a glorious Divine pattern for just human behavior that has shaped so many laws and so many societies since. The Decalogue clarifies justice, telling us that we shall not steal. We can't just take whatever we want. We shall not even want (covet) another person's property or wife. This means the standard extends to the human will itself, which if left unchecked will certainly invent all sorts of evil means to serve itself. It is injustice to leverage our physical, economic, social, or legal power over others to benefit ourselves or to remove someone impeding us from getting our way. We shall not kill; we shall not bear false witness.

We are to uphold justice through submission to the law, even when that law means we lose some advantage or power over our neighbor. Furthermore, when we find ourselves disliking the consequences of this just God, we do not jettison the One, True God in favor of ourself or a god of our own making, who might allows us to live as we please. We shall have no other gods and make no idols. The way the law is integrated into the lives of the people of Israel is through the institutions of family, tribe, and kingdom and incarnated in cultural forms in every sphere of life. The ways of God's commandments are trustworthy, and they are designed for life to flourish for all, including the poor.

There were also beautiful policies that were instituted to extend justice into economic and other spheres of life. We are to give laborers, and animals, and even our own bodies a weekly sabbath of rest. We are to grant the ground a sabbath every seven years, not incessantly demand, extract, and consume resources. We are to leave the gleanings at the corners of our fields for the landless poor, rather than collect every bit for ourselves. We are to tithe to support those who give up the means of production to serve the community in the temple. We are not to charge interest in our loans to each other. We are to honor our parents when they are no longer economically productive. When they are an economic cost to the farm, and a burden to the household, we gladly support and take care of them as they carried us in our poverty and infant vulnerability.

Most amazing of all was Jubilee, a restoration of property every 50 years. This is a policy that both acknowledges and actively combats the natural progression of disparity. Some by reason of unequal capacities or resources or the results of good crops, would prosper; while others might suffer a string of bad turns, an illness, a poor yield, exploitation in the market, accumulation of debt. And so they might be forced to sell their land or even indenture themselves in labor to their neighbor. The people of Israel were not to enslave each other. In the year of Jubilee, the Sabbath of Sabbaths (the year following seven sevens of years), they would restore the freedom of the indentured poor and restore the land and its fruitfulness to its original owner. This regular leveling ensured the people of Israel would have a unique constraint on prosperity and poverty. This unique constraint in turn was a tangible way in which Israel could extend its blessing to the world as a sign that disparity is not inevitable. If justice is active and practiced, life could be different. The extent that they lived by the law of God, was the extent to which Israel demonstrated the uniquely Just Heart of God in their society.

What is notable about the shift to the New Testament is that the tenor of God's message about justice does not change. The aim of the Kingdom of God is still life in all its fullness, as God intends, which is most definitely not an unchecked life of benefits for a few and exploitation for the poor. Christ said he did not come to destroy, but to fulfill the law. In his life, he was the model and means of justice, the blessing of all nations that Israel so frequently failed to realize. Christ was Jubilee. He was the messenger of good news to the poor and freedom for captives, a New Covenant, which comes, not by means of an external law of justice, but by rebirth of humanity in the Spirit of God through their identification and communion in Christ's death and resurrection.

This was prophesied in the Old Testament. God promised he would do a new thing: he would plant his law in peoples' hearts; he would replace our heart of stone with a heart of flesh (making reference to a kind of law that was not just written on stone tablets but on the tablets of our hearts). Christ was able to institute a kind of inside-out transformation that the law could not fulfill on its own. Precisely because it is external reveals the limits of legal justice. There have always been plenty of examples of people exhibiting all the right external behavior in conformity to external signs of sanctification and laws, but whose hearts are far from God. "You pay tithes of mint, dill, and cumin, but you have disregarded the weightier matters of the law: justice, mercy, and faithfulness" (Matt 23:23).

In Christ's teaching about the Kingdom of God, he invites us to take the law of God into our hearts. He extends the standard beyond mere avoidance of injustice to active redemption. In this way, he demonstrated his power to not just offer an external check on injustice, but provided a way to kill and undo injustice. If injustice spreads virally and compounds every time it is passed on, Christ was able to show that the place it must die is in the hearts of men, not just by sinlessness, but by forgiveness and active love. Christ raises the prospect of the restoration of true human government ("the government will be on his shoulders") and the redemption of Edenic stewardship. Such is only possible if our hearts were changed, if we were able to both desire and do what is good and just (Phil 2:13). This kind of love of law and law of love is only possible if we are reborn by the Spirit of God, and indeed take on God's heart for redemptive justice as our own. Internal justice is only possible in the work of Jesus Christ, and so we must not only receive his justice as a gift, we must receive his person as the agent of justice in our hearts.

The world has yet to fully see the fruits of that transformation. In fact, we are told that the world is groaning in anticipation of the revelation of the children of God, as the whole created order will receive its redemption through our transformation and revelation. How else could the earth and its inhabitants be properly and thoroughly restored, apart from the healing and restoration of its marred stewards? The sub-agents of God's intended justice need to both be redeemed and to become the agents of redemption. Is that not the most thorough of reigns, to take back not only the earth, but the hearts of men, since we have been the chief agents of unchecked lawlessness whose consequences are ubiquitous in the earth?

In God's Kingdom, we are told that the futility we were subjected to will no longer reign. Humans will no longer have to take care to defend ourselves in a competitive kill-or-be-killed, dynamic. Rather, righteousness and justice will reign. The most powerful signs of that coming justice in a society, in an organization, in a family, in any institution, is the flourishing of the most vulnerable. What must be done to ensure the flourishing of the most fragile flowers in God's human garden? When and where the little ones live and thrive together with the strong, without fear, in spite of their weakness, there justice governs. And "the wolf shall dwell with the lamb...the child will put his hand over the adder's den" (Is 11).

Ancient Roadmaps
Martyrdom emboldens us to witness to those who will join us in this way of poverty, as well as to testify against the ways of the world.

The Discipline of Martyrdom

The word martyr simply means witness. It represents a chief function of the disciples of Christ in the world, simply to testify to the good news of the Kingdom of God and thereby testify against the kingdoms of the world. Martyrdom has obviously taken on an association with death, as we think of Christian martyrs as those being willing to witness to the Gospel, even when it costs them their lives. We tend to think of martyrdom as a special case for the great Saints and Apostles of the faith. And indeed in 1 Corinthians 4:9 Paul says that God has ordained death for the Apostles. They are to be a spectacle for the world, angels, and men and be offered up like Christ as a public offering to the community of faith. There is no doubt of the special calling that God places on some to literally give their lives for the Gospel. However, in some sense we also know that martyrdom is for all, not just for special cases.[2]

Christ Jesus said to them all, "if any man will come after me, let him deny himself, and take up his cross daily, and follow me" (Luke 9:23). And more strongly he states again, "And whosoever does not bear his cross, and come after me, cannot be my disciple" (Luke 14:27). The calling of Christ is the Way of the Cross. Our death might not be a public execution. It might be a death of our own self-will, or a death to our power to get our way, or a death to our consumption, but following Jesus will always entail some kind of cross. These are not to be confused with all the ordinary burdens we bear due to the vicissitudes of life; our crosses are the deaths that we willingly take up in the following of Christ. These are the deaths that are the natural consequences of identifying with Christ and others marked for death. If I say, "I am with him; I am with them", and they are being dragged to death, then what follows logically from the act of solidarity is my own cross.

However, we do not go looking for deaths; we do not need to. In the context of contemporary injustice, any degree of alignment of our words and lives to the Gospel will bring death because it misaligns with the structures of the world. A witness for Christ is inherently a witness against the powers that be. If the world devalues the handicapped, the unemployed, the refugee, then there is no greater act of defiance than to counter that system with love. We need not shake our fist at "the man" when forgiveness, tender care, and self-sacrifice will shake the world's

---

[2] Tertullian *Ad Martyras* 3. Cyprian *Epist.* 10.5

values and structures to the core. When we show up the world for what it is (a place of injustice), they will come for us, and they will bring many kinds of death with them (John 15:17-27).

We must be clear about the nature of our witness, however. It is very tempting when we suffer injustice to counter with violence. But to return evil for evil is only to multiply it like a virus. We can only overcome evil with good. In this way, forgiveness is the chief means of martyrdom. We declare that this hurt will not multiply; I will not pass it on; it dies within me. "Father, forgive them, for they know not what they do" (Luke 23:34). That is clear in the case of injustice to ourselves, but how are we to respond to the injustice done to others? In this we witness through meekness as well. If we try to counter power with power, we merely affirm power. "The wrath of man worketh not the righteousness of God" (James 1:20).

If on the other hand, we counter power with self-sacrifice, we end up inserting our selves in between those who suffer and those who harm. We may not attack, but we can offer a buffer, a human shield, willingly offering various aspects of our resources, our lives and even our bodies to suffer the violence already raining down on the vulnerable. Of course we will catch flack if we are prepared to go in harm's way, and that is why non-violence is essential to Christian witness, because it affirms our belief in Christ's promise that the meek shall inherit the earth. "And they overcame him by the blood of the Lamb, and by the word of their testimony; and they loved not their lives unto death" (Rev 12:11).

To be meek, however, does not mean we run away. The act of "opting out" of the world in some sense needs to take place right in the heart of that world, the arena. Christian martyrdom in the Roman arena was a public event of witness within the context of the civic community. For us as well, martyrdom means checking out of the world, right in the middle of the world. Actively defying the values of the world, right in the face of the world, by living the values of the Kingdom of Love in the world. We are not to seek a platform. The choice is to be in the world but not of it, remaining and not abandoning the vulnerable while choosing to live out the justice of another Kingdom.[3]

---

[0] Pucci, Michael C. "Aronao" in *Dictionary of New Testament Background* (Downers Grove, Ill.: InterVarsity Press, 2000).

We need to restore martyrology. The Christian tradition of martyr stories is very old. But perhaps we have forgotten the importance of martyrology, the recounting of stories of those prepared to die for their faith. Without such heroes how else are we to know how to die well? We need the witness of martyrs, backed up by their deaths, to stir us up to courage to face even our little crosses. However, today we cannot even tolerate the thought of failure, let alone physical death. Our Christian bookstores and business leadership programs are full of stories that all end in glowing success. We overemphasize winning and are thereby diminishing the Church's capacity for martyrdom. We need to be shown how to fail well, how to lose well, how to be humiliated well. We need martyrology restored in all arenas of life, if we are to have the courage to join wherever we are placed in that faithful witness unto death. Imagine, for example, what a martyrology of Christian business might look like. Instead of how to become a billionaire, it would teach us how to keep our integrity even when it means betrayal and bankruptcy.

We need to restore covenants. To counter injustice, we do not need more wristband marketing campaigns as much as we need more authentic relationships of promise keeping. We need to bind ourselves to others for better or for worse, in sickness and in health, for richer or for poorer, to love and to cherish till death us do part. We need to extend these kinds of covenants that make marriage possible, beyond marriage to all of life. In marriage, as in any covenant, we are not seeking death, or poverty, or illness. What we are saying is that we will faithfully remain in that relationship, regardless of the outcomes and costs. We are saying that our mutual commitment to maintain the relationship is not contingent upon our safety, our wealth, or our well-being. And when the other suffers one of these poverties, we own it as ours. In the inevitable choices set up between love and life, we choose love above life.

There is no need to manufacture an artificial sacrifice. There are thousands of real hills to die on, to which our solidarity with the poor will lead us. And being in real covenant relationships with them will reveal what things we must give up, what deaths we must die, in order for the beloved to live and to receive life in Christ. In relationships of love, shared poverty is the authentic medium of witness, and there are some contexts where power and wealth and everything else must be stripped away in order for us to remain true to love. In certain contexts, the poverty of death is not only the most effective vessel of the Gospel, it is the only way the love of God can be witnessed to with integrity.

Practice: *It seems a strange thing to call martyrdom a discipline, to say that we need to practice death. However, every small death prepares us for greater, and builds our faith in the death and resurrection of Jesus Christ. Every little endurance from love is also a token of his great passion. In our witnessing through little voluntary deaths, we identify with Christ and join him in the fellowship of his sufferings and we identify with all those who suffer injustice. There is no greater act of solidarity, no greater love, than that we lay down our lives for our friends. 1. Find and read the story of a martyr of the faith. 2. Make a small commitment to someone this week where you know keeping your promise will likely cost you.*

Questions: Poverty & Injustice

Guides
Checks & Balances
Can you think of a time when you have seen God provide a merciful external check on your own injustice or sin?

Companions
Inside Out
Is law working only from the outside upon us or is justice at work within?

What are some ways in which the spiritual disciplines of privation can cooperate with the Holy Spirit in writing his new law of justice on our hearts?

The Lion and the Lamb
What is the place of diversity and fragility in creation, in the Kingdom?

Where does justice demand we intervene to preserve space for the weak rather than allow the domination of the socially, legally, physically, and economically strong?

Journal
What happens (to others and to me) if I start with my own desires, wants, and needs as the measure of what is good?

What decisions is God's Spirit urging that I make to check my own lust and consumption?

POVERTY & TRANSFORMATION

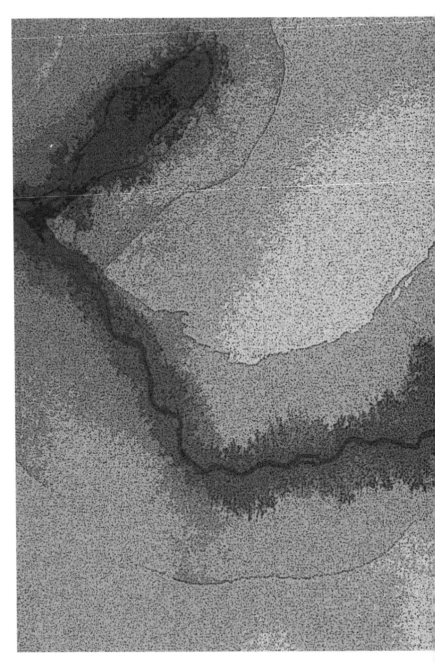

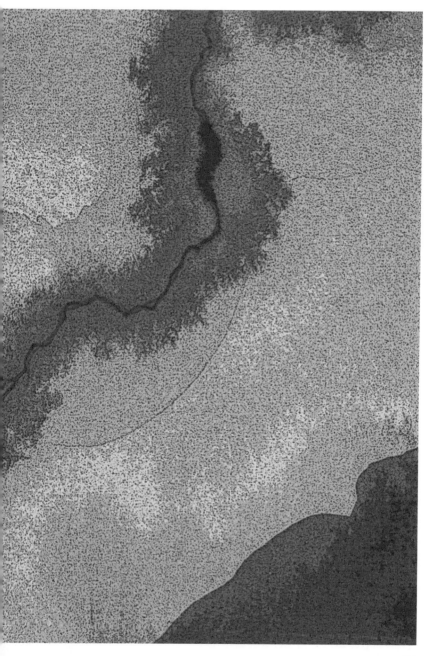

Taking a Bearing

The depth of ongoing transformation in me may be proportional to the breadth of transformation God is able to facilitate through me.

The medical missionary, Paul Wilson Brand, pioneered surgical work with those suffering from Hansen's disease, a bacterial infection more commonly known as leprosy. Before Brand, it was widely believed that those suffering from leprosy lost their fingers and feet because of rotting flesh. Instead, Brand discovered that such deformities were due to the bacteria effecting the nervous system and causing a loss of the ability *to feel pain.* Imagine how much damage you would do to your toes if you couldn't feel them. With leprosy, even the most minor bumps, scrapes and bruises do not receive healing from the body, and become quite seriously infected and damaged, because they are ignored. The healthy feedback is interrupted. The body is unaware; it simply cannot feel its extremities and loses connection with its members. Applying lessons from medicine to life Brand explains, "From pain-deprived people I have learned that I cannot easily enjoy life without the protection provided by pain."[1] Pain lets us know when something is wrong. A pain-free life, which some people pursue as the ideal, is actually a condition that facilitates death and decay, because everything that is wrong, goes unnoticed. Absence of any pain is not life-giving, but rather an indicator of disease that is life-threatening.

Suddenly the horror dawns on us that the Church in the global north is likely suffering from spiritual leprosy. We in the body of Christ should be very concerned that we cannot feel our finger being smashed in Sudan, our foot broken in Burma, our thumb starved of lifeblood in Honduras. We are one with those suffering right now. If we see nothing, feel nothing, and do nothing, how can any spark of health remain, let alone the love of Christ dwell in us (1 John 3:16-18)? Lord, have mercy on us, for if the diagnosis is correct, I fear this condition may prove fatal. Already there are so many hurts that go unnoticed and have definitely become infected. Can I suggest a necessary component of treatment? What is required first of all is an examination of the wounded parts, for example, an extended visit to a church where the majority of its members are refugees or who are dying from AIDS or suffering of famine. Such an examination may not restore feeling automatically. Christ alone must heal that atrophied capacity in us, but this visual awareness may be a start, and it is a prerequisite to healing that we acknowledge how bad our condition is. Plus, when those in spiritual poverty and physical poverty are reunited in the body of Christ, a unique mutual healing becomes possible.

---

[1] Brand, Paul and Philip Yancey *Pain: The Gift Nobody Wants* (Grand Rapids: Zondervan, 1993), 289.

Now imagine what it must have been like to be healed by Jesus of leprosy, to not merely have the visible, physical blemishes and the social stigmas removed, but to have full feeling restored. It would have been wonderful but also rather overwhelming to suddenly have your nerve endings come alive. To flesh out the metaphor, the true healing of our spiritual leprosy, not merely the removal of the outward signs like disparity, or the shame of our isolation from our own body in Christ, but the miraculous, full restoration of our capacity to feel and to love, is no doubt a completely transformational, but also particularly painful experience.

For those from a culture that mistrusts emotion and avoids pain, the intense hurt, sadness and often anger that tokens that miraculous restoration of feeling, gives all the signs of something bad. Why, if this change is a good thing, do we feel *more* pain? But this amplified emotion is evidence that we are actually beginning to process reality again, by integrating it through our whole person, mind, body, heart, spirit. Like the sensation of running water over frostbit fingers, initially there is no nuance of feeling, no hot, no cold; there is only undifferentiated sharpness of pain, until proper feeling is fully restored.

So far, this might well describe the sensations of the immediate post-transformational trauma. There are also new sensations and feelings that linger and seem to be communicating feedback from new realities deep within. Our sadness seems to say, "Yes, this poverty is real, and it is hurting me. It will affect me now in a way it couldn't before because it has come inside me. I don't know how that happened. It must have gotten in there via those people whom I have grown to love. This painful reality was a part of their life, and now they have worked their way into my very heart. And so they have acted like carriers, bringing that very thing I was trying to avoid, poverty, deep inside me. The only way to get rid of it, is to get rid of them, and it is much too late for that. So this reality residing deep in my gut can only be acknowledged and felt." And Jesus wept.

Charting a Course
Read Mark 2.

In Mark chapter 2, Jesus is asked why his disciples were not fasting like the disciples of either the Pharisees or John the Baptist were fasting. Jesus' response is curious. He answered, "How can the guests of the bridegroom fast while he is with them? They cannot, so long as they have him with them. But the time will come when the bridegroom will be taken from them, and on that day they will fast. No one sews a patch of unshrunk cloth on an old garment. If he does, the new piece will pull away from the old, making the tear worse. And no one pours new wine into old wineskins. If he does, the wine will burst the skins, and both the wine and the wineskins will be ruined. No, he pours new wine into new wineskins" (Mark 2:19-22). In essence, Jesus answers the question by stating that the paradigm had shifted. Sometimes, the old ways aren't sufficient to accommodate the new destinations, the old signs aren't sufficient to signpost the new realities. In this example, Jesus even goes so far as to say that trying to go on pretending as if the new doesn't change the old, can end up ruining both. This principle holds true in our journey into owning poverty as well.

As you begin to reintegrate into your old life and culture, you will be made more aware of much that God has taught you and ways he has transformed you through this pilgrimage journey. The contrast with the places you left, which did not change in the same ways, will remind you of what has changed in you. It's possible that you may even have seen God at work in ways that you've never seen him work before. It is helpful to think of all your collective experiences and lessons of poverty as "new wine" of experience. If you attempt to take these fermenty truths and place them in the "old wineskin" of daily routines or the old wineskin of how you used to relate to God or the world around you in the past (simply conforming to the way life is done back home) it's probable that your new realities will burst out of the old you, and you will find things unravelling.

The intentional crafting of a new vessel, a new life, capable of expanding to accommodate the new wine, is a necessary component for ongoing transformation, and bringing to fruition in your life what God started in a cross-cultural context. It is also the hardest part. It takes a lot of integrity, tenacity, and prayer to be real in a place that can sometimes feel like Disneyland.[2]

Owning poverty is a point of integrity for all followers of Christ. It takes integrity to not deny our dependency on God, but proclaim it in our lives and words, especially to a world that idolizes self-sufficiency. Unless we own our poverty, how can we testify to the fact that God is with the poor, in our suffering and in their suffering? Our spiritual eyes have been opened to discern the hand of God at work in the midst of the incredible poverty in our world today. If we now close them, what will we have to say to those who question God's whereabouts in human experience?

Your understanding of poverty has changed. You now know in a personal way, with names and faces of friends involved, that the reality of human experience is, for the vast majority, excruciatingly hard a lot of the time, and for all, hard some of the time. You have also grown to realize how

---

[2] Stringfellow, William. *An Ethic for Christians and Other Aliens in a Strange Land* (Waco: Word Books, 1973). Hauerwas, Stanley & William Willimon, *Resident Aliens: Life in the Christian Colony* (Abingdon,1989).

relevant the Gospel is to this reality. Are you prepared to continue to personally walk with the poor and have your own capacities transformed in loving engagement with (and for) those in poverty, so that your life and words will be a true signpost of what God is doing in his Kingdom? The assertion of the goodness of God in the midst of human evil and poverty is a statement of faith that is reinforced by joining him in his incessant incarnation in hard places of suffering.

God is interested and intimately involved in all manner of transformation, not just invisible, interior change, but spiritual renewal in all actions and transactions, in behavior, posture, and habits of individuals as well as in cultural structures and institutions. He is the God who made all things, and he is bringing it all back under the Kingdom of his Son. Jesus Christ is the transforming inaugurator of the redemption of all things visible and invisible, present and future. And the ongoing transformation of our poverties is a prerequisite to discerning and facilitating transformation of the poverty of other individuals and communities, in humility and with the eyes of faith, hope, and love.

As we begin to craft new wineskins, new actions, new habits, new lifestyles, new livelihoods, new life-giving liturgies, we do the work of affirming and nurturing the transformation God began and wants to finish in us.[3] We give it the space it needs to grow. We needn't fear whether what he is calling us to signpost is normative in our home culture or even if it has never been done before. We are compelled by love to see these changes through to fruition. With God upholding us and accompanying us, we need not fear what we are becoming or where he is taking us. Jesus told Nicodemus, "The wind bloweth where it listeth, and thou hearest the sound thereof, but canst not tell whence it cometh, and whither it goeth: so is every one that is born of the Spirit"(John 3). You may find that others from your home culture also say this of you "I'm not sure where you're coming from or where you're headed with this whole 'owning poverty' thing."

Ancient Roadmaps
God is the sole Agent of transformation and calls us to hope for and signpost his Kingdom.

The Discipline of Hope
This study has been downright repetitive regarding the necessity of grieving for owning poverty. We do not go through life wearing rose

---

[3] Sherrard, Phillip *The Sacred in Life and Art* (Limnia: Denise Harvey Publishing, 2004). Durrwell, Francis Xavier *In the Redeeming Christ* (Paris, 1960, Notre Dame: Christian Classics, 2013).

colored glasses, pretending that everything is fine. To grieve is to articulate (often through tears or clenched teeth) that things are not the way they are supposed to be.[4] While this is necessary and good, it is incomplete without hope. To only see what is wrong, without hope, brings despair. Hope is believing that things need not be the way they are, that they can change, and that in fact, through the transformative agency of God, they *will* change. We are part of Christ's Kingdom which has been inaugurated through his death, resurrection and ascension, and which has been planted in the church through his Holy Spirit. However, the Kingdom is not fully revealed. It is both "now" and "not yet."[5] That means that an essential component of hope is its capacity to see what is present but invisible as well as those things that are still to come.

Hope then is a function of prophet imagination. For it is the faculty of our imagination which enables us to picture the future, and it is the future image shaped by God's promises, which characterizes the prophetic nature of our hope. We are not looking forward to just any old future, but rather, we anticipate the new heavens and new earth in which Christ reigns completely. All three of the following are essential for keeping the embers of hope burning in a dark world. In order to hope we must:

1.*Actively imagine and seek Christ's promised Kingdom everywhere*
2.*Train our hearts to wait in full expectation of the promised fulfillment*
3.*Participate with the Spirit to incarnate foretastes of glory here and now*

The discipline of hope for personal transformation
What happens when we apply this to ourselves? We know "everyone who is in Christ is a new creature, old things are passed away, behold all things have become new" (2 Cor 5:17). If I were to only behold myself in the mirror with my earthly eyes, I would despair to see the difference between what is described as a new creature and my sinfulness. Should I then conclude that it is not true, because I cannot see my own transformation? No. I must acknowledge my sin, but I understand my transformation in Christ to also be "now" and "not yet." My transformation is a present (but not always evident) truth that I must therefore see with the eyes of hope. Who I am in Christ and who I will be in glory is a fact, but I also have a role in realizing that transformation here and now. John explains it this way, "Beloved, we are now the children of God, but what we shall be has not yet appeared, but we know this, that when he shall appear, we shall be like him, for we shall see him as he is. And everyone that has this hope in

---

4Plantinga, Cornelius *Not the Way It's Supposed to Be: a Breviary of Sin* (Grand Rapids: Eerdmans, 1995).
[5] Mouw, Richard *When the Kings Come Marching In: Isaiah and the New Jerusalem* (Grand Rapids: Eerdmans, 2002). Tadie, Andrew A., and Michael H. Macdonald Eds. *Permanent Things: Toward the recovery of a more human scale at the end of the twentieth century* (Grand Rapids: Eerdmans, 1995).

him purifies himself, even as he is pure" (I John 3:2-3). What is very clear here is that hope itself is a key factor of transformation. To hope in transformation is to participate in the Spirit's work of purification. To fail to hope, is to fail to imagine who we will be in the beauty of his Holiness, and to fail to anticipate its complete fulfillment, keeps us from believing it is possible to begin realizing more of that glory in our lives today. We are changing from glory to glory, becoming like him as we behold Christ's image. And when we finally see him fully, we will also be revealed fully as the children of God. We will know as we are known, and that knowing will, like light, pass finally unimpeded through our whole person, leaving no part in darkness, no occlusion unpenetrated by his brilliance. This glory he will share with us for all eternity.

It is like his love lifts us onto a pedestal that is far above where we were, and the power of his word over us (which spoke the world into existence, by the way) has the power to remake us into his lovely children. So our hope is not in ourselves but in "him that is able to keep us from falling, and to present us faultless before the presence of his glory with exceeding joy" (Jude 1:24). That image that just flashed in your mind, of a glorious creature whose face is reflecting the light of the glory of Christ, without blemish and shining with the (still allowable) tears of joy, that image is you. That is a glimpse of your destiny, your future. Hope helps "that you" to begin breaking through into the visible world, even now.

The discipline of hope for community transformation
Our transformation would not be complete, if it were purely solitary, internal, without any manifestation in our behavior, relationships, and environment. Through the incarnation of the Kingdom in our lives, we individuals multiply transformation in the lives of other individuals. However, community itself is essential to our transformation. Transformation entails our restoration as beings in right communion with God and others. But is transformation of larger institutions possible? It seems that even the transformation of many individuals is in itself insufficient to bring transformation to culture and structures of society. For this God has created the church, the body of Christ, to be the institution that witnesses to (and against) the institutions of the world. As with persons, it is effective in transformation, only in so far as it is salt and light. If it is no difference, then it merely reinforces the structures of injustice in the world. But Christ has shown us how his body is to be sanctified. As with our personal transformation, it is easy to despair of the church ever becoming what she is called to be and what she must be, for the world to receive grace through her. Unfortunately, the church more frequently mirrors the power structures, the leadership styles, the

economics, and the relationships of exclusion of the world rather than the Kingdom of God. However, we are not allowed to write off the church. There is no external vantage point from which we can sit on our high horse and judge the church; we are her members. Nor can we conceive of the goal as being our personal transformation, regardless of the outcomes of transformation of the church or of the communities in which we live. It is not a very deep transformation that would allow us to be content with our own personal rescue and perceived righteousness, while the church sleeps and injustice prevails in the world.

There are so many in our churches who do not get it, and we would just prefer to exit and not have the life sucked out of us by engaging those communities. However, if we are to participate in her glory, we must own her poverty as our own. Her sins of commission and omission throughout history are ours, and the gap between how she appears and behaves and what she is spiritually, and what she will be in perfection, should cause us to love her and contribute to her transformation, rather than abandoning her to avoid association with her sins. Hope will not allow us to leave her, and love will not allow us to tolerate anything less than her perfection. Hope causes us to not give up but to adorn her in holiness. We must exercise the discipline of hope in order to see the church as the chosen vessel of Christ, whom he will prepare as his spotless bride. In hope we fully expect Christ to reign in the church and shine his light through her. In hope we ask God to gift us for the equipping of his church and through her, the transformation of the world.[6]

Herein is a mystery in the relationship between individual and corporate transformation. Our destiny is bound up with the transformation of the whole body of Christ. Furthermore, our fruitfulness in God's work of transforming the world is also proportional to our own ongoing transformation. In order to be a part of God's ending of poverty in ourselves and the whole world, we must own it. We cannot be content until "the whole earth is filled with the knowledge of the glory of the Lord, as the waters cover the sea" (Hab 2:14).

---

[6] Yamamori, Tetsuanao & Rene Padilla, *The Local Church, Agent of Transformation (Buenos Aires: Kairos, 2004).Walter Brueggeman, The Prophetic Imagination, 2nd Ed* (Fortress Press, 2001). On the restoration of imagination to its proper place in Christian spiritual formation, see MacDonald, George, "The Imagination: its Function and its Culture" in *A Dish of Orts* (1867).

Practice: We must exercise prophetic imagination to clarify the visions of the Kingdom that God gives us. This week, ask God to give you a vision of one transformation in your own life and one transformation in your own church community that you hope for. One common form to incarnate this hope is the practice of **watching**. This means staying up without sleep throughout the night in prayer and imagining what you are hoping for. Instead of merely critiquing what is wrong, describe and picture what should be. What would things look like in their newly transformed state? Flesh out everything that could be different from the way things are now. Once you can begin to see it in detail, in hope, pray for it. Ask God to bring transformation, and to continue to renew hope and give us ways we can participate with him in bringing about his Kingdom.

Questions: Poverty & Transformation

Guides
New Wine in New Wineskins
What are some examples of ways you have incarnated new wine into new wineskins?

Are there examples when you needed to craft new lifestyles, habits and cultural forms into your own life because you had changed significantly?

Companions
Signposting the Kingdom
Are there examples of others you admire that seem to signpost Christ's Kingdom in unique ways?

Why is hope such a difficult discipline for us?

Journal
Healing the Lepers
Am I able to identify areas where God has restored feeling in me, healing my spiritual leprosy and renewing my capacity to love? How would I describe that sensation?

What do I really hope for?

Have I taken the time and energy to imagine and to seek first the Kingdom of God and his justice?

REFLECTIONS & CONCLUSIONS

Now that a foundation has been laid, we need to think about what relation owning poverty has on our past, present and future.

Owning Poverty is Naming Transformation

The first of these reflections requires looking back and taking stock of your own transformations. In the significant changes we experience, we witness the hand of God. God is, in fact, the only agent of transformation. Through the in-dwelling work of the Holy Spirit, he seeks and effects our well-being and our ultimate good through our transformation into the image of Christ. To admit and hope in that transformation is to cooperate in his purification. When God grants us the grace to see glimpses of his deep work in us, we should mark and record those times and give credit to God (where it is due). To name transformations sharpens our capacity to see by faith more of what is really going on (II Kings 6:17ff).

However, we often lack the language to identify and articulate precise changes and end up generalizing with phrases like, "that experience of poverty changed my life." In reality there are many kinds of change. Small changes at the surface can be frequent occurrences in our lives. Those are often much more difficult to attribute correctly (a change in behaviour could derive from something as mundane as what I ate for breakfast this morning). But changes in deeper things give a strong and clear indicator that something has happened that only God can do. It is helpful then to describe the kinds of changes we see happening at varying "levels". The following "Levels of Transformation" framework gives us more differentiated language to talk about the changes we have been experiencing in the Owning Poverty journey. You will likely find that the process of describing these changes (and the episodes God used to bring them about) also helps to clarify them and bring them into focus. The very act of speaking an interior truth, can be an act of revelation, when we discover who we have become. If naming something also gives it renewed power in our lives, then Divine transformations are indeed the best sorts of things to name.

Practice: Take some time to explore the different levels of transformation. The levels progress into deeper and deeper modes of change and are accompanied by questions designed to help us identify and name those important changes. This reflection is meant to trigger memories of specific experiences that reveal or point toward God's work of transformation. As much as possible, describe specific events, people, places, and examples as evidence of the changes you are naming. In this way, you will provide yourself a record of transformations for future reference when the immediacy of these experiences fade.

Levels of Transformation

Awareness — What have I seen that will stick with me?
Are there things I observed in new contexts that were hard to process or that were so strikingly beautiful they are now etched in my memory?

Knowledge — What have I learned?
Are there new facts or realities that disrupt what I used to know?

Behaviour — What is different in my actions?
Are there any new cultural forms I have picked up or new habits forming?

Beliefs — What new things have I come to believe about God & his world?
Are there things I thought I 'believed' before, but now I *really* believe because they have been strengthened by the faith of others or a new experience of God?

Values — Who and what is important? How have my life priorities changed? Are there indicators that things I used to value have less currency or my weights and measures of success in life have changed?

Authorities — How do I interpret the world differently?
Are there indicators that where I go for answers is shifting (e.g. away from self and toward the Word, Christian community, the Holy Spirit)?

Posture — How do I approach God and others?
Are there differences in the posture of my prayer life (e.g. more begging, urgency, simplicity, gratitude)? Is there evidence of greater willingness to receive grace, greater willingness to submit to God and others?

Capacities — What can I see, feel, tolerate now that I couldn't before?
Are there poverties in myself or others that I can see now that were invisible before? Are there miraculous new capacities (to grieve, to rejoice, to hope, to trust, to love) that simply weren't there before? Are there new capacities to hold onto things that do not make sense, to wrestle with complexities instead of avoiding or 'solving' them?

Identities — What or who have I taken inside my definition of who I am?
Are there changes in my solidarity with the body of Christ, with humanity? Are there new free expressions of generosity with my time, my things, my self that seem to call to question the very sense of that word 'my'? Am I sensing fearless movement into new Kingdom relationships?

Spirit — What new spiritual hungers are evident?
Are there new thirstings and cravings for holiness, for justice, for mercy, for love?

Owning Poverty is Grieving

Secondly, we desire to prepare those who have sincerely engaged in this study with their head, hands, and heart for the emotional processing of owning poverty. Processing is not a way to memorize the emotional aspects of transformation and then try to sidestep them like landmines. The desire to get all the benefits of transformation but avoid the messiness of our feelings mostly comes from a Western mistrust of emotions. However, if God intends to transform all of us, he is not going to by-pass our hearts. In this journey there is no *around,* only *through*.

The key message to hear is that emotional processing is part and parcel of owning poverty, not something abnormal or something that can or should be avoided. And emotion will be, is bound to be, expressed somehow. Self awareness and intentionality are the best outcomes we can hope for. Self awareness leads to a greater degree of respectful holism in our engagement with ourselves, as opposed to a mechanistic paradigm that treats the self as an object to be controlled or programmed. We are not machines that we fine tune to perform to task by ignoring or suppressing our emotions. Rather, we are creatures, made in the image of God, whose hearts are integral to who we are and become. Our emotions are not to be treated as disruptive nuisances in performance-driven lives. The first 'goal' with our emotions then, is normalization, to see that what we are feeling powerfully is to be expected. The second is intentional stewardship, to treat our feelings as gifts and valuable assets in our lives and in the Kingdom.

We acknowledge that transformation entails meaningfully integrating new, sometimes jarring, truths into our very persons. We have tried to take in a lot on this journey, and it is no easy thing to process poverty. Everyone processes differently and at different rates, but there is a framework we find useful to take an assessment of where we are at in our emotional processing at any given point on the journey. You may be familiar with the model called the "Grieving Process". Although designed as a way of framing the common experiences of those having to adapt to the realities of death, we have found the principles apply well to other difficult truths that we encounter and are forced to incorporate somehow into our lives. It is particularly helpful when our experiences cause us to encounter painful realities, like poverty and injustice. In processing the reality of poverty, we are in fact bombarded by the normal human emotional responses to traumatic grief: denial, anger, bargaining, fear, and sadness.

In reading the following descriptions of the different typical phases of the grieving process, you will probably find that you can identify times during your journey where your emotional experiences resembled that response.

It is good to identify those times in your journal. However, it is more important to try to describe the phases you most identify with *right now*, at this moment in your journey. The nature of emotions is immediate, which is to say, processing is more effectively focused on what you are feeling now, than the memory of feelings.

Practice: Preferably with your Owning Poverty companions, discuss all of these phases, then put yourself into groups according to where you identify yourself now. Discuss why you believe that phase aptly describes how you are currently feeling and processing the painful reality of poverty.

DENIAL
The first phase of emotional processing, denial, is the natural reaction to something difficult. "It is in a sense the only interior crisis worth talking about. It is that in which every nerve of the body, every consciousness of the mind, shrieks that something cannot be. Only it is."[1] Denial can take many forms.

Delusion—is denial that pretends this painful reality simply does not exist. This kind of poverty, inhumanity, just can't be...so it isn't.

Deafness—is denial that refuses to hear the truth, like children sticking their fingers in their ears and chanting "la, la, la, la: I can't hear you." The more adult version is, "I'm just not ready to hear that right now." We may find ourselves at times even physically unable to hear what we deny.

Blindness—is denial that refuses to look at a reality. We shield our eyes or look away. At times we can't see the poverty right in front of us.

Numbness—is the condition of denial characterized by not being able to feel what we should. Like those who have lost sensation in their fingers and toes, we in the body of Christ experience numbness in our feeling for others. It is normal to experience momentary neuropathy (pins and needles) once in a while. But neither we nor the rest of the body of Christ can remain healthy in the unfeeling condition of spiritual leprosy.

Escape—is another symptom of this emotional state of denial, seeking to remove ourselves from difficult emotional states. Reinforcing a worldview that insists we should always feel good, the entire drug industry provides a chemical approach to a pain-free condition, addicting many in the process. We have developed many other drug-free methods, to assist our emotional escape into other moods, which often create equally addictive attachments to behaviours that temporarily deny the bad feelings.

---

[1] Tho great poets like Shakespeare are the only ones who come close to expressing the outrage. Williams, Charles *The English Poetic Mind 1932* (Canada: Distributed Proofreaders, 2010).

The urge to lock up poverty in a black box and bury it away from our hearts, and to run as far and as fast as we can in the other direction, can be strong. Denial is a normal emotional response, and an important, often necessary, stage to pass through. Everyone needs to escape now and again, to find distance from painful realities. However, we do not flourish if we stay in denial.

ANGER

The next common emotional response after denial is anger. Anger is an emotional attempt to defend ourselves by taking the offensive.

Blame—is an outwardly directed expression of anger. With something as complex as poverty, we usually aren't too particular about who gets blamed. We blame all authorities: government—why aren't they doing anything about this?, the church—why are they so apathetic and complacent?, previous generations—why have they messed things up so badly?, my teachers—why haven't I been taught about this?, God—how could he allow such things to happen?, etc. If we are not careful, we can end up pointing our finger or shaking our fist at everyone and everything. Any authority in range, even innocent bystanders can receive the brunt.

Rage—is when anger behaves like an emotional fire, flaring up in us, even when we are not aware we are angry. Our companions may be able to attest to this, even if we don't recognize it in ourselves. Especially in cross-cultural or reentry contexts we may find ourselves exploding at the smallest of things, in anger very disproportionate to the trigger. This of course gives us lots of scope for repenting and receiving forgiveness.

Bitterness—is the result of directing our anger inward and bottling it up. This may be complicated by self-blame or cultural norms about non-expression. Over a prolonged period, unacknowledged anger turned inward can eat your insides like a cancer.

Activism—is anger finding legitimization through a cause. One can discover that actions (even in categories labeled as good activities inside Christian organizations) are motivated by anger. It is not uncommon to find motivations for 'service' infected by an anger at God's perceived absence. We act as if we are stepping up to do what he has failed to with his world. Such actions are not really going to do us or the poor much good because they will eventually turn to resentment. Activism will not replace the honest conversation that needs to happen with God.

The key is to be transparent about our anger, which is often difficult to do in non-expressive cultures. The Psalmists got it right with their emotional transparency, when they expressed so much anger in word and song and offered it undisguised upward to God. They knew God is not afraid of and is able to handle their anger. They also affirmed that God is not fooled by duplicity and instead hears us when we pour out our true hearts to him.

BARGAINING

After anger comes the bargaining phase. This response tries to make a deal with the universe, with God, or the Devil, or ourselves, inside our own minds, so that this new reality (which granted, now exists) at least does not come near to us and our loved ones. "O.K. so I'm not denying poverty and exploitation are real; they have made me very angry, but surely there is a way to make sense of it and to contain it. What do I need to do to guarantee what I saw others suffer will not happen to me?"

Mechanistic Theology—is a way of bargaining to manage the spiritual realities of poverty. Let us say that the gap between horrible sufferings in the material world and the glory of the promises in Christ is finally acknowledged and felt. For some, it is best explained away in a kind of spiritual reductionism. The reasons for poverty they locate in individual spiritual causes. "The reason anyone is not experiencing a glorious one-to-one correlation between their spiritual and physical condition must itself be attributed to the spiritual cause of sin or lack of faith. If they only believed correctly, then all would be as it should be." It is of course, heretical, not to mention emotionally unsustainable, to say victims of genocide, rape, slavery, displacement, starvation, simply did not pray or believe hard enough or that they weren't the right sort of Christian for God to rescue.

Prosperity Gospel—is one brand of spiritual reduction infecting Christians with a pagan theology of appeasement. To attribute a lack of healing or lack of wealth unilaterally to sin or disbelief is not the message of the Gospel. It is the message of Job's friends, whom the Lord rebuked. They could not conceive of a God who would allow suffering in a good man... but there he is. Bargaining tries to answer "why?" to the outraged mind by providing reasons and rules. This heresy attempts to bargain our way back to a universe in which we predict and control the agents of poverty.

Fear—is of course the root of bargaining. And fear is a threat to our allegiance to Christ. For if we find that the real God won't bargain, fear amplifies the temptation to deal with others who will promise more control over outcomes. The essence of idolatry is the adoption or creation of our own gods who will work for us and deliver reality according to our terms. We may spot this when we try to bargain with God. "If I do this, will you keep me prosperous and safe?" In that very act it is clear we are attempting to speak to some other god. That feeling of being mentally exhausted by one's own incessant efforts to orchestrate everything ourselves, to reduce reality to the point where it all makes sense again (with or without God), and to ensure that everything works out O.K. for me and mine; that is a strong indicator you are stuck in the bargaining phase.

SADNESS

Sadness is evidence that we are actually finally beginning to take the reality of poverty inside, integrating it into our inner being. For those from a culture that mistrusts emotion, sadness, like anger, is also seen as a negative. The painful reality of poverty that I was trying to avoid, is now deep inside. Here is this world in which the rich, those chief perpetrators of destruction, are the last to be effected by the consequences of their crimes against humanity and their environmental injustice against communities and creation itself. Instead, the vulnerable are the first and primary ones to suffer, to hunger and be starved off of their land, to be displaced, driven from their homes and countries, to be excluded, demonized and jailed like criminals, their children caged like animals. Those with low economic power are traded and trafficked as human cargo, exploited and spent, treated as valueless, disposable, and ultimately eliminated, aborted, murdered, and slaughtered in war. A rescue of the weak from the strong oppressor, a lifting up of the lowly and a putting down of the proud, a safe place for all in community, this is what justice demands but is absent. I have spent my anger at the injustice and now I begin to touch my own powerlessness to bring any good from myself to right these wrongs. Instead I find in myself the seeds if not the causes of the injustice I despise. Human poverty is much worse and much deeper than I thought, and I am overwhelmed in a sea of sadness.

Depression—is an extreme form of sadness, which is persistent and saps us of our motivation and begins to take over and shut down life-giving systems. It is a natural reaction to go into a dormant, winter phase of low maintenance in order for the body and soul to recharge and rebuild. But we need to watch for evidence of depression, namely, when things we normally do to recharge are not effective. When sleep fails to reenergize and reboot, when food does nothing and we lose appetite, when relationships fail to fill us, when our spirit forgets to hope, and when we get locked into mental messages of despair, sadness has tipped into depression. It is difficult to tease apart the physical, emotional, and spiritual aspects of depression, and not always helpful to try get down to its causes. It is clear that depression requires outside help from friends and counsellors to help us reimagine and restore hope. It is also a significant comfort to know we are not alone in what we are wrestling with. During deep sadness, we need to seek out companions who will accompany us on the journey without trying to fix our feelings. We also need to become that kind of a friend to others.

ACCEPTANCE

Acceptance is not meant to describe some zen state that represents the absence of powerful feelings. On the contrary, acceptance is in many ways both coming through each phase and the change in capacity to continue working through the phases of the grieving process. Acceptance is our capacity for compassion growing larger rather than a reality-denying complacency. It is our capacity for active love growing larger, rather than angry activism. It is our capacity for faith growing larger, rather than a fearful fatalism. It is our capacity to identify with the sufferings of others growing larger, rather than a diminishing of our hearts in despair. Acceptance isn't so much arrival in the journey as it is a deepening in our experience of painful truths. It is also not a linear progression, where we tick off the phases like steps. We can often find ourselves processing in more than one way or cycling back and forth between phases. There is always something more of poverty to take deeper into our selves and to integrate into our lives. Consequently, acceptance looks like movement toward greater internalization and greater expression of poverty, whereby we continue to ask if we are currently saddened and angered enough. This points to the possibility of conceiving of our emotions as not just necessary but valuable. How would we and others engage in good without emotion? How could any justice be effected or maintained if injustice is not felt? It is this interior, heart work of owning poverty through which the hard work, the long, slow, persistent defeat of poverty is sustained.

Owning Poverty is Refining our Faith

Let us walk back through this whole transformational process. From the comfort of a quiet stasis of our ordinary thoughts and lives, buffered by self-protecting theologies and economic theories, we are thrust into an encounter with the experiential realities of poverty. We are stung deeply by a truth now raining down on our heads without shelter. We are powerless to even describe our state, and all attempts, (even those we have offered in this study) seem unfit to the task. "Grief call it not—anything but that, A conflict of sensations without name." We are struck dumb, blind, and paralyzed by what is but should not be. "The world is executing an appalling outrage on our whole being."[2]

---

[2] Williams, Charles *The English Poetic Mind 1932* (Canada: Distributed Proofreaders, 2018). The Shakespeare quote is from *Troilus* 10:263ff.

A study like this, especially accompanied by second-hand experience of extreme poverty in others, seems to wreck our whole world. And the fact is, there is no guarantee of the outcome of an encounter with poverty. From the encounter comes an outrage; from the outrage comes a change. The transformation could be conversion; or it equally could end in apostasy. The thing they both have in common is trauma, a trauma that God can use, but a trauma nonetheless. One argument is that encountering the realities of poverty causes people to doubt their faith, so we should avoid it. However, one must question which faith is being doubted and exactly what faith we might be losing in the process? For nothing but faith in the real God will withstand the onslaught of reality. Every other faith, in any other god, religion, theology, system of thought, even if it calls itself Christian, will not stand. When our worldview is shattered by poverty we sense the personal fulfillment of the word that now God is not just shaking the earth but the heavens as well (Heb 12:26).

These days atheist arguments are not typically about reason or science, but are directly related to owning poverty. They ask, "what kind of god could allow such evil?" The question may be honest; the conclusion that there is no God, is an extreme form of bargaining. It is like removing the tension of a knot that is proving impossible to unravel by just cutting the rope. There is certainly emotional resolution in ceasing to oscillate between denial, anger, bargaining, and sadness, but at great expense. If we conclude that no God of justice exists, and no non-subjective good exists to be outraged about, then there is only human nature and human power to appeal to. Whoever has power gets to define the good, and ultimately might-makes-right. So the foundation for one's initial critique of might-makes-right injustice in the world and a god who does not intervene to uphold true justice, seems to be undermined by the conclusion of atheism. Human evil has still not been redressed, but rather accepted without any recourse to divine justice. It doesn't make sense to shake our fist at a god, who in the same breath we say doesn't exist. It might be better to start by simply admitting we are angry. The root of our anger is the "what kind of a god, god" failing to behave how we believe justice demands. When such a god ceases to "function" predictably, we become indignant, despite the fact that those injustices, in many of which we share guilt, were preexistent to our knowledge and to our indignation.

Many think God's response to such doubts would be to silence us, to tell humanity to stop questioning his goodness and power. But Job, the archetypal questioner, is blessed by God, and his friends who had "figured out" God were told they had better ask Job to pray for them. Part of the emotional satisfaction of bargaining often entails answering our own questions before we get a true response that we might not like. If we are really sincere about seeking answers from God, then shouldn't we actually wait for his response? We may find that the response includes a few questions from God as well. "Gird up your loins like a man; I will question you, and you declare to me. Will you even put me in the wrong? Will you condemn me that you may be justified?"(Job 40:6ff).

Instead of disdaining our outrage, or silencing the questions, God deigns to dialogue. The Almighty Creator actually responds to Job as the representative of creaturely indignation. His response is a long resume of God's care for and care-taking of creation. God points to the fact that along with his care, he has the knowledge and the power to execute justice for all of creation. His challenge to Job asks you and I also to prove that we match him in the power or the will to do justice. "Deck yourself with majesty and dignity; clothe yourself with glory and splendor. Pour forth the overflowings of your anger, and look on every one that is proud, and abase him. Look on every one that is proud, and bring him low; and tread down the wicked where they stand. Hide them all in the dust together; bind their faces in the world below. Then will I also acknowledge to you, that your own right hand can give you victory" (Job 40:13ff). We are the little ones, whose station is dwarfed by many mighty creatures on the earth and the sea and sky whom we cannot understand let alone command. So how will we, in all our anger, bring justice on earth or to those above in the heavens? We who exist in the blink of all that has been created, when did we become the great champions of justice? We imply that we can either do better than God or we can at least imagine better. In a loose paraphrase, "if you are all about justice, then let us see you roll up your sleeves and get 'er done. Or if you just have better solutions for the injustices caused by human and diabolical agency, then let's hear this counsel of yours to the Omniscient…about things you have just learnt."

God reminds us of the limits of our power to know and to do anything about poverty but also the limits of our care, the very thing that is fueling our (honestly felt) critique. It seems until we have personal skin in the game, like Job (or like Abraham, who had family in Sodom and Gomorrah) we tend to remain unconcerned. "Oh, so you have felt the injustices done to and by humanity? Do you think you are informing me or instructing me about something that I am unaware of? Teach me then. You care? Good. I have always cared, I have been caring about this world long before I made it, and I have not once ceased to care about all of it, including obscure things that still have never crossed your finite mind. But it is nice that your own participation in poverty has finally caused you to care about some aspects of it. I have also had a hand in your caring, and your newfound hunger for justice, as well as your very anger for injustice. Previously you were not even willing to think about my wrath at the exploitation of the weak. If you really do begin to care about poverty, as your feelings indicate, we finally have something to talk about now, you and I. You want me to do something about it? Good. I also want you to do something about it. You're serious? So am I. So let's get to work. Shall we begin with some injustices within your reach, say, right there in your heart?" God is not at all interested in silencing us. On the contrary, he is about something far more dangerous—transforming us. God is actively initiating our care, even our outrage, and wants thereby to draw us deeper into his heart. But people who don't care also can't be shocked, angry, sad, and confused. The question is, are we prepared to lose our own care and distance ourselves from the God of care in order to turn off those 'hard' feelings?

So if an encounter with poverty, even second-hand, causes us to doubt our faith, perhaps it calls to question what we had faith in previously. Was it the God of infinite care and justice, who took our suffering into himself in Jesus Christ? If our faith demands that we be taken care of, that no harm comes to me and mine, that only bad (other) people suffer, then for sure, an encounter with good, Christian people suffering evil at the hands of others, without immediate rescue, shakes such faith. You see now why the grieving process is apt, because the absence of a divine guarantee of freedom from suffering human poverty, and the outrage of our powerlessness to change that, are as difficult to process as death itself.

I do not recommend one try to preserve one's naive faith in a god who can only be said to care if there is an absence of suffering in those he loves. It will just result in more bargaining. For the "what kind of a god, god" that cynics describe, simply does not exist. And we would do well to lose faith in that construct as quickly and thoroughly as possible, in order to clear a path for an encounter with the true God. We are also right to lose faith in an animistic god whom we appease to guarantee us good things. Along with that, we need to lose our faith in delusions like the prosperity gospel, Christian triumphalism, the American dream, and so many other idolatries in order to find true faith in the God of the Cross. The fact that our faith is being tried (refined) is normative. "Beloved, do not be surprised at the fiery trial that has come upon you, as though something strange were happening to you. But rejoice that you share in the sufferings of Christ, so that you may be overjoyed at the revelation of His glory" (1Pet 4:12ff).

The incessant temptation to equivocate on the substance of our faith, to believe in something or someone else other than the person of Jesus Christ, be it ever so "Christian" in name, is the essence of the trial. We are rightly told to pray for God to lead us not into trial but for him to deliver us from the evil one. Without divine grace our faith will not withstand the trial. Temptation offers many shiny substitutes for our trust in the will of God, including guarantees of basic needs, happiness, safety, power, stability, predictability, prosperity, control, etc. Those all sound good until we remember who is making those offers, namely, the father of lies, the one who told our parents, that we would not surely die. He told similar lies of power to Jesus Christ who resisted him in the desert with fasting, prayer and God's word. Poverty was Christ's ally then and continues to be our ally of true faith. It shines a light on how false and fragile are the constructed alternatives promised by temptation.

Owning Poverty is Abiding in Christ

If our faith demands prosperity, safety, triumph, then we will forever be scandalized by our encounter with the suffering God. This is why the first foundation of owning poverty is always identification with Jesus Christ in his poverty. "In order to believe in him one has to begin with his abasement."[3] Christ himself has also told us we that we reject or accept him through our identification with "the least of these" his poor brethren (Matt 25:32ff). Abiding in him means taking up residence and identifying with those with whom he was not ashamed to associate. The essential question of Christian identity then is, are we (still) *with him* and *with them*? "If you cannot bear this contemporaneousness, cannot bear to see this sight in reality—if you cannot prevail upon yourself to go out into the street—and behold! it is God in that loathsome procession; and if you cannot bear to think that this will be your condition also if you kneel and worship him: then you are not *essentially* a Christian."[4]

What does it mean to have allegiance in the Messiah who claimed to be God while hiding in poverty and suffering all the experiences of the lowest poverty? What are we to make of his way of the Cross, the scandal of all scandals, and outrage of all outrages, this God prepared to and able to suffer? We prefer to rush ahead to the glory. We tell ourselves we would not have been among the scoffers who rejected the Nazarene, but here we are today lightly rejecting his poverty. We claim we are not rejecting his poverty, but the poverty of others, those others who surely are cursed of God and who must 'deserve' their poverty—things which they also said of Jesus. But how can we say we love God whom we do not see when we do not love our brother whom we do see? We cannot separate the two, Christ and his (chosen) poverty. To attach ourselves to something or someone else, to align with a visibly triumphant god, or a god untouched,

---

[3] Kierkegaard, Soren, "The Preparation for a Christian Life" in *Selections from the Writings of Kierkegaard*, Trans Lee M. Hollander (New York: Doubleday Anchor, 1960), 181.
[4] *Ibid.*, 211.

unpolluted by poverty, that is not the faith of Jesus Christ, but rather the spirit of antichrist. "For many deceivers have gone out into the world, refusing to confess the coming of Jesus Christ in the flesh. Any such person is the deceiver and the antichrist"(2 John 1:7). One way to deny Jesus Christ came in the flesh is to claim that he only appeared or seemed to be man, but was not 'really' human, not fully sharing the human condition, including participation in the real experience of poverty, the unknowing, the hunger, the disparity, the exclusion, the powerlessness, the subjection even to death.

To disassociate with Christ's poverty is to deny both the realities of our own poverty he came to ransom, and to deny the conditions of Christian faith in the lowly Redeemer. There are many who have shaped Jesus the Son of Man and Son of God, into a power idol that serves their own formula of poverty avoidance. But it is this Immanuel, this God with us in our poverty, who is the real stumbling block. Those who have grown up in the church are often buffered from feeling that offense of Christ's poverty, his "Blessed is he whosoever shall not be offended in me." Some for whom it might be considered cultural, even respectable, to be a Christian, do not understand the offense or the social stigma of associating with the one who was despised of men. "Let us also go forth, therefore, unto him outside the camp, bearing his reproach"(Heb 13:13). We are prepared to identify with the idea of Christ, whose poverty was historical, with the finished priestly work of Christ, whose poverty was spiritual, with the glorified Christ, whose poverty was eschatological. But any real acquaintance with experiential poverty, with his *being* poor, homeless, of low reputation, irreligious, outcast, shameful, criminal, powerless, easily killed, and we flee. The shepherd is struck, and we the sheep, like his first disciples, are scattered. It is not like we actually lack opportunity to identify with Christ in the poor. We must ask if by rejecting poverty we have really accepted his Gospel to the poor on its true terms. Owning poverty "is ever reminding one how the Christian must suffer in order to become, or to remain, a Christian—sufferings which he may, if you please, escape by not electing to be a Christian."[5]

Owning Poverty is Obeying Christ

Let us then dispense with the notion that poverty has nothing to do with Christian faith or that we can get it at a bargain. These days the trial of our allegiance to Christ will frequently be framed as the choice between alignment with the powers and values of the world, which promise us protection from poverty, versus alignment with the powerlessness of the

---

[5] Kierkegaard, Soren, "The Preparation for a Christian Life" in *Selections from the Writings of Kierkegaard*, Trans Lee M. Hollander (New York: Doubleday Anchor, 1960), 211.

cross and the values of the community of Jesus Christ. We are mistaken if we believe we can have the Christ without his poverty, precisely because his salvation is hidden in poverty (Matt11:25). It also doesn't make sense to say that our faith in the lowly one and our identity with the wretched ones will require no jarring separation from the world. "Religion that is pure and undefiled before God, the Father, is this: to care for orphans and widows in their distress, and to keep oneself unstained by the world" (James 1:27). Bruggemann's commentary unpacks this best. "'Defilement' is caused by participation in the desires of the world that eventuates in an indifference to orphans and widows. This sequence of themes—riches that perish, desire that leads to death, generosity rooted in God, and actions toward the resourceless—taken together, constitute a teaching that contradicts the easy assumptions of the world: that wealth endures, that desires should be satisfied, that generosity is foolish, and that religion has nothing to do with real socioeconomic need."[6] Such 'defiled' religion is unfaithful to Jesus Christ, perhaps is no faith at all.

If on the other hand we are Christ's and with Christ, we share his blessing on the poor in spirit, the poor of heart, those with a posture of poverty, as we identify in our spirit with the poor. In order to identify with the poor, with the powerless, not only must we choose non-violence but frequently choose renunciation, the non-use of wealth and power in its many forms. In this respect, we have learned that there is nothing magical about the statement, "blessed are the poor." The poor are blessed in the same way the lame and blind are blessed. There is nothing inherently holy about physical poverty. Poverty is an evil that devours the life and seeks to undermine the God-given dignity of the person. The blessing is that physical impoverishment alerts the poor to the human powerlessness we all share. And since we must all come to faith through that poverty, the thing that disadvantages the poor in this world is an advantage in finding the Kingdom.

Only in light of the reality of Christ's Kingdom does it make sense to call the poor blessed. We must acknowledge our empty-handedness to receive the gift from God. None of us can bring anything to the bargaining table with God. We are absolutely bankrupt, morally and spiritually. The real blessing of the physically poor is the preparation their life gives them to grasp and receive more readily the truth about our spiritual poverty. They are able to assume the correct and authentic posture of a beggar that the Gospel requires of us all but which repulses so many of us who would like to think we are doing just fine. The hardship of poverty removes

---

[6] Brueggemann, Walter *Money and Possessions,* Interpretation: Resources for the Use of Scripture in the Church, (Louisville. Westminster John Knox, 2016), 251.

the veil, the lie, that we ever had any sufficiency in ourselves or in anything other than God. The means of faith itself is a poverty, a trusting, equalizing unknowing that puts us all on the same level.

That same word of poverty in the Gospel seems to speak one thing to those experiencing material hunger, and another to those who have material wealth and believe they are not in poverty. "He has filled the hungry with good things, but has sent the rich away empty"(Luke 1:53). We should not be surprised at this dual nature of the sign. Christ came to give sight to the blind and make blind those who see. He came to heal the lame but said those who pronounce themselves well have no need of a physician. There is tremendous mercy in such a Gospel that confronts our delusions. If human poverty is our true condition, then we will need the sign of physical poverty to remove the veil.

This sign of poverty is a hard word for the rich who have so many things reinforcing their delusion. But do not miss it; the sign of poverty given to the rich is (potentially) just as liberating as the pronouncement of blessing to the poor. To treat the condition of the materially rich man as anything other than a bondage—the only difference being that the chains of the rich are of gold and they have grown fond of them—is to disconnect from reality as God names it. Not only does God call the poor blessed, but calls the rich truly poor and in jeopardy of losing the gifts of life and the Kingdom. If Christ calls the rich, poor and at risk, we need to take his word for it rather than operate as if things are as the world defines them. In this respect the sign of owning poverty, as incongruous as it sounds, is redemptive even for the rich.

Owning Poverty is Incarnating the Kingdom

Finally, we can begin to turn our reflections towards living out or incarnating our transformation. We begin with a warning not to spiritualize what we have learned from God in our encounter with poverty. Any attempt to rationalize poverty away or whitewash poverty, or diminish the experience of poverty in others, or contain our own poverty response to a pietism in our interior life, will have missed the point and departed from the way of faith, hope, and love. We know that poverty affects the whole life of the poor, robbing them of health, education, choice, and the freedom of mind and heart to imagine and build a different life, as well as the voice to defend themselves from exploitation. Imagine how ridiculous it would be to conclude that owning poverty invites us to identify with the poor, but only in our minds, sending them warm, happy thoughts and prayers, as it were (James 2:16). Owning poverty is not meant to be a means to spiritual narcissism, focusing on my own brokenness as an excuse to ignore the brutalities others are suffering. "If you know that he

[Jesus Christ] is just, you know that everyone who practices justice has been born of him" (1 John 2:29). Owning my poverty propels me towards the reality of the universal need for God's grace, which as I receive it, frees me to become both a sign and an operative of the Gospel of the Kingdom proclaimed to the poor. Transformation seeks to bear out the truth of poverty in fruit in our lives.

That is easier said than done. For we barely understand what the word transformation means and we have no words at all to describe the springs of action that come from that change. Many have a kind of "Magic Eight Ball" view of change, believing that if we just have the correct beliefs in our head and just shake it about, then the correct response will float up effortlessly and be expressed in word and deed. However, "There is not a simple cause-and-effect relationship between "faith" and "works", but "rather the Spirit's actions in the midst of the community that continues to profess "Jesus is Lord" is the cause, and the effect is spiritual gifts that manifest "good deeds" performed as ongoing allegiance (1 Cor. 12:1-3)."[7] Owning poverty resists the separation of inside and outside, life and economics, spiritual and physical. The authority of Christ's Kingdom will also not be contained to one sphere of life. Authentic incarnation of owning poverty requires a much more intentional and involved process of alignment of our insides and outsides to each other and alignment of both to God's insides and outsides, revealed in his Spirit and his Son.

Practically speaking, owning poverty involves taking further steps to engage in community transformation, working to advocate for the most vulnerable in your communities at home (the alien, the prisoner, the widow, the orphan, the homeless, the unemployed). Some may be called to prepare for owning poverty in cross-cultural contexts by going to live and walk with those in extreme poverty. It will not be enough to launch a few good intentions. Cross cultural servants of Jesus Christ need to commit to the painstaking task of translating faith, hope, and love into visible signs of the Kingdom and will need to demonstrate a propensity to demonstrate the transformative power of the Kingdom on their own culture and lives first, for all to see. This all will require work of immense imagination, courage, planning, and humility.

The testimony of the early Church captured the centrality and potency of poverty in the Gospel of the Kingdom. The realms of the spiritual and physical met and merged in the redemption of each person; the realms of the ecclesiastical and economic merged in the expression of the Kingdom

---

[7] Bates, Matthew W. *Salvation by Allegiance Alone: Rethinking Faith, Works, and the Gospel of Jesus the King* (Grand Rapids: Baker Academic, 2017).

in community. There were miracles, healings in the physical sphere, emancipation from sin in the spiritual sphere, reconciliation in the social sphere, as well as miracles of generosity in the economic sphere. The Lord of love kept reordering the 'rings' of their priorities to testify to the presence and quality of the Kingdom. Christ told them that the world would know they were his disciples by their love. Love in and amidst poverty was to be the evidence of his Spirit in his body. We are no more able to extract or exclude God's sign of owning poverty from the Kingdom than exclude the other divine signs like sacrificial blood atonement.

Owning Poverty is Being Witness

Owning poverty reveals something at the heart of what is good about the good news. It openly declares how bad things are, and proclaims that God is not happy with the *status quo.* He has ushered in a new Kingdom, and has used his own right hand to bring salvation (Psalm 98:1-3). Some pretend that human evil and suffering is an illusion. Others try to make the measure of evil relative, pretending that injustice is only a matter of perspective. Still others profoundly miss the relationship between sin at the micro level of the human heart and institutionalized evil in social, economic, and cultural structures at the macro level. The Kingdom of God says otherwise. The powerful language of poverty is employed throughout scripture to shed light on our human condition and the Gospel that remedies it, not least of which is that great constellation of signs in the prophecy of Isaiah that Christ fulfills. "The Spirit of the Lord is upon me, because He hath anointed me to preach the Gospel to the poor; He hath sent me to heal the brokenhearted, to preach deliverance to the captives, and recovering of sight to the blind, to set at liberty them that are bruised, to preach the acceptable year of the Lord" (Luke 4:18).

If it is true that the medium is the message, God is certainly saying something very profound about the nature of the message of the Gospel of his Kingdom. For he has chosen to send us. When God wanted to speak the truth in fullness, he sent his Son in person, in poverty. Now the Gospel is the word of God in us. We incarnate the Kingdom because we are sent as God's medium of choice. The human medium is not just a nice to have, it is the best vehicle for the Gospel. For the Gospel is not a law or a disembodied message that God wants to convey, but the living, breathing covenant of the Kingdom exampled in its messengers. If the Gospel is good news to the poor, it is also good news through the poor.

The Gospel of the Kingdom belongs in persons for the same reason and in the same way that God chose to express the truth in the man Jesus. To overlook the role of our persons in poverty as the carriers of the Gospel is to run the risk of skipping over essential qualities of the Gospel medium.

He has chosen the weak things of this world to confound the strong. Chosen. Those sent by God are not like independent insurance agents for the Gospel, working on commission. We are not independent of the Christ of the Gospel at all, and we who are sent cannot be separated from the message – the glorious riches of this mystery which is Christ in you, the hope of glory (Colossians 1:27). We are to be the message and medium in one, word in person, truth in life. And we are the best expressions of both the poverty of the human condition and its redemption and ongoing transformation in Christ. The Gospel is not some objectified message that some paperboy delivers but never reads. It is this amazing light and life, glory and truth that confronts, breaks and heals the messenger *en route*. We thereby provide both show and tell to our audience. We are never a disinterested, third-party observer of the facts of the Gospel. How could we be? We and they need more than some facts about a change in status due to Christ's work. Rather, the world needs to see the power of God in the poverty of those who believe.

Therefore, the fact of our imperfection as vessels of the Gospel is something we need to embrace, not hide. It is precisely our sharing in poverty that makes us effective priests. Furthermore, walking in a posture that acknowledges the truth of our own poverty is itself alignment with and testimony to, the power of the Gospel. Our Gospel is actually Christ's Gospel, and so it should not surprise us that it is in weakness and poverty, in vulnerability and solidarity with the poor, that we witness. And yet we tend to hide the very poverty God wants to heal and wants to become the sign he uses to communicate the power of the Gospel to others. Our posture of poverty should communicate the true nature of our relationship to the Gospel as recipients of great grace. The authenticity of our transparency as God continually reveals and heals our poverty is a powerful vessel of the Gospel. By owning poverty there will always be fresh material for our testimonies. The Reformation writers understood this principle as *semper reformandum*, always transforming. We limit the testimony of the Gospel when we confine it to a single point in time in our lives. We thank God for continuing to reveal our poverty, for we have never ceased to need his mercy. And we can no more complete our transformation than effect our own conversion or resurrect ourselves.

Owning Poverty is Choosing an Identity

We must not remain in doubt about the nature of God's posture, despite the lies we may have been hearing that material prosperity is the sure sign of his favor. "Has not God chosen the poor in the world to be rich in faith and to be heirs of the kingdom that he has promised to those who love him"(James 2:5)? If we are convinced, then we must shun the spiritual imperialism that claims those who have prosperity and security are blessed and those who don't must be cursed, leading to further rejection of the poor and God himself.

We must stop avoiding poverty. We must instead own up to our own poverty and our own part in inflicting poverty on others. We must own the suffering of those whom Christ calls our brothers and members of his very body. We are one with those suffering right now. If we see nothing, feel nothing, and do nothing, about that body, how can the love of Christ dwell in us (1 John 3:16-18)? We must allow the sign of physical poverty to reveal our spiritual poverty and pray against the spiritual leprosy currently infecting the body of Christ.

We must not deny our dependency on God, but proclaim it, especially to a world that idolizes self-sufficiency. Unless we own our poverty, how can we testify to the fact that God is with the poor, in our and their suffering? Unless we train our spiritual eyes to discern the hand of God at work in the midst of the incredible poverty in our world today, what will we have to say to those who question his whereabouts in human experience? We must also not allow the complexities of our world's poverty to paralyze us but allow the Gospel to have its fruit in every sphere of our lives, especially the long-neglected economic sphere.

The assertion of the goodness of God in the midst of human evil and suffering is a statement of faith, which is reinforced by our joining him in his incessant incarnation in poverty. All blessings multiply in the sharing, and all sufferings divide and diminish in the sharing. So we must give, and we must receive until we are utterly confused about which one is which. We must not just give to the poor and maintain our status above them. We must go live with them. We must bring them to live with us. We must embrace into our inner circles those whom God calls blessed, whom the world does not even remember, let alone love. It should also be said that the benefit of our living and walking with the poor is not chiefly theirs but ours. For there is nothing more grounding, nothing that recollects our true condition of utter dependence on God. And we will long to go there because Christ is already there among the least of these.

If you are wondering why young people who grew up in Christian homes are "less engaged" in the faith these days, it may not be the truth of the Gospel that bugs them; but perhaps the lack of integrity to the Kingdom that Gospel proclaims. Young people want to hear and experience *more* of the real Kingdom at work, not less. When you observe through their 'idealistic' eyes, you can see how much of the church's energy and voice are spent maintaining and justifying a friendship with the world that Christ calls adulterous enmity with God (James 4:4). Contemporary Christians find themselves deep in the grip of market ideologies and too deep in the pockets of the world to offer concerted resistance through a differentiated physical, spiritual, social, and economic expression of Kingdom values. It should grieve us that so many of those claiming a Christian heritage have succumbed to the slow, invisible bribe of economic conservatism. We are also tempted by the subtle micro idolatries of self as savior and haunted by the macro idolatry of reliance on human society. To escape all this in order to incarnate the Kingdom will quite simply take a miracle. But we should not be surprised when young people expect more of Christianity than an invitation to join a little suburban, gated community, and instead seek ways to live their faith that signpost the miraculous Spirit of God. Bless them in their journey deeper into owning poverty, especially if it is a trip older generations have grown too comfortable to take.

I can certainly imagine the flack the next generation might get for the idealism and foolishness of this sign of owning poverty, especially from older Christians. Are we really prepared to let our children go live with the poor? Prudent advisors are always saying things like, "that would be such a waste of potential". By saying that aren't we claiming, contrary to the Kingdom of God, that we ourselves, our dreams and aspirations, our plans for the future, are more important than, worth more than, those of the poor? That faithlessness to what our Lord actually says, seems to be the root of our attempt to separate the resources and hearts of young people from the poor? We must be careful that our 'protection' does not incur the wrath of Christ who said, "But woe to you, *religious leaders and teachers*, hypocrites! For you shut people out of the kingdom of heaven. For you do not enter yourselves, nor do you allow those to enter who are trying to go in" (Matt 23:13). With regard to incarnating the Kingdom values, Christ anticipates the saying, "lead, follow, or get out of the way."

I can imagine the difference it will make to both the integrity and the power of the Gospel when a generation is found fearlessly owning poverty. I can imagine what it might mean for them to be free from those economic fears that paralyzed us. In full confidence of the safety net of God's infinite love, even now they are beginning to do some amazing trapeze acts, while the prudent are still hugging the pole. Once imagined, I am no longer able to get that shining vision out of my mind. So I appeal to the older generations and ask what they really wish for. Do we really hope that the young have what we have, only more of the same, our fears, our delusions of safety, our slavery to the *status quo*? Surely it is natural to hope for better for our children. I do not fault the instinct; our definition of 'better' just needs radical revision, from a life of material prosperity our culture calls good, to a true picture of the Kingdom, of which we claim to be citizens.

Even when we ourselves lack the courage to proclaim our faith by doing the words of Jesus Christ, we still must declare his true Kingdom values. Woe to those who are prepared to preach some other Gospel so that they come out smelling like roses. Indeed we do proclaim that all persons have undisputed, equal worth as the beloved of God, all persons including the poor, 31 million of whom are currently in slavery, 70 million of whom are currently refugees and displaced by violence and competition for resources exploited and spoiled by the rich, and 35,000 of whom die every day from hunger. We confess their worth, and we confess in the same breath that we have not lived by the reality of God's gracious love for them, but have been defiled, hijacked by the world's value system. To proclaim this is step one in restoring our allegiance to Jesus Christ.

Poverty is far from a peripheral or neutral issue of the Christian faith; it is a central sign, one that continues to resist reduction or avoidance. Poverty is both something God cares about in itself and something he uses as a sign (in ways we cannot reduce) to point and to reveal. This sign of poverty images the helplessness of our estate and the way we all must receive the Kingdom of God. It tells the truth about the common condition of the poor to whom the Good News is preached and holds up identification with the poor as integral and necessary. Poverty is a double-edged sign, a call to both the materially impoverished and to the rich of this world. The value system of both the rich and the poor are radically overturned by Jesus Christ. Poverty speaks the message of a new Kingdom economy characterized by Christ's justice. That justice is intended to be planted in Christian hearts and cultivated to work a lasting and fruitful transformation in and through us to all of creation. Poverty is meant to be lifted up as a sign by his earthly body, the Church. Following Christ's example, a posture of poverty is right and fitting for all messengers of God's Good News to the poor. The reality of the gift of grace emboldens those for whom Christ became poor to deeper and fuller ownership of poverty, spiritual and physical, their own and others'. Owning poverty becomes a testimony for those who will receive our message as well as a witness against those who will not. Regardless of the reception, we await in hope the redemption of all things in Christ, a restoration of the pattern of his glory, which is the fullness of his justice and mercy, the end of poverty, the conquest, destruction, and displacement of all unjust forms and modes of power, the final eschaton, in which the kingdoms of this world have become the Kingdom of our Lord and of His Christ (Rev 11:15).

AUTHOR'S AFTERWORD

The reader should know that at a personal level I have wrestled with the necessity of this journey of owning poverty. I have helped to facilitate many encounters involving incalculable trauma: a mother calculating the economics of trafficking her daughter into prostitution, a refugee calculating his rations, a pharmaceutical company calculating the unprofitability of drugs for the poor, development planners calculating lives they can't afford to rescue. One moment that captures my own struggle was a time I was guiding university students through the horrific realities of the genocide against the Tutsis that killed a million people in Rwanda. We were visiting the site of a church where those seeking refuge were slaughtered in the sanctuary. One young American woman in our group was visibly broken and sobbing at the outrage. I remember praying to God through my own tears and asking him if this was what he wanted me to do. What was the good of facilitating breakdowns?

Two things happened next which were important. First, unable myself, I asked our pastor and course lecturer to pray. There followed the longest, most awkward pause at the beginning of prayer, which ended up finally containing just two words, "It happened." The truth of poverty, with its accompanying outrage and trauma, is preferable to the lie that it didn't happen, that injustice doesn't exist, that it isn't so bad, that others' suffering doesn't matter that much, or that we had better just let the beast lie undisturbed. The truth, the reality of human evil, craves the dark, but cannot remain covered indefinitely. It happened, and the light reveals it.

Our encounter with a previously ignored poverty may entail our emotional trauma at the new realization of both the extent of human potential for evil and the extent of our obligations and responsibilities. Ignoring evil to avoid its emotional costs and practical demands was the self-same posture that in fact implicated us, the international community, in the failure to intervene in the Rwandan genocide or to even name it as genocide. To fail to name poverty is a failure to defy the world's view of the worthlessness of the vulnerable; it is an assent to the futile value system of "every man for himself," and "better them than me." If we see and say nothing because we don't like how it might make us feel or what it might require of us, then we are saying there is probably no alternative, no such thing as the Kingdom of God and his justice. Owning poverty refuses to hide or minimize the evil in the world and in our own human hearts.

The second thing that happened was like one wounded by poverty hearing the good news proclaimed to the poor for the first time. Our guide at the memorial, a Rwandan genocide survivor, who lost her family in that slaughter, took this young woman to her bosom like a child and began stroking her hair to comfort her. The genocide victim was comforting *us* in our secondary trauma! It was as if, in this woman, God himself, the true Comforter, was comforting our sorrows in a way that revealed he is more deeply acquainted with our suffering than we can imagine. For me it was an unveiling of the Kingdom, a true image of how comfort and redemption must come in a real world that cannot simply erase or wish away evil. All of our tears will be tenderly wiped away in a similar manner by the true Sufferer. And here was God coming again, as he always does, lowly and into the midst of our poverty to bear for us what we truly cannot. "His place is with those who do not belong, who are rejected by power because they are regarded as weak, those who are discredited, who are denied the status of persons, tortured, exterminated. With those for whom there is no room, Christ is present in this world. He is mysteriously present in those for whom there seems to be nothing but the world at its worst."[8]

It also revealed that the only real comfort is God himself. Only he is enough. I desire him to come to bring true comfort to everyone. I desire it with all of my person. And if someone wanted to find that God, I have no better advice to give them than that they should look where he always is, about his Father's business, bringing comfort to the afflicted, in person. But he is also the God whose offer of comfort must meet us in our true condition, the condition requiring comfort, in fact, in our poverty. So what must I say? I cannot wish for anyone to avoid poverty and thereby miss out on true comfort. And if a multi-faceted experience of poverty like what we have been exploring is part of other's becoming poor in spirit, then "Let the brother of low degree rejoice in that he is exalted, but the rich in that he is made low" (James 1:9ff). These desires clearly implicate me deeply in the hope to see many more people owning poverty.

As you will have gathered, this process of owning poverty does not end with this introductory study. If you would like to go deeper, explore more resources, practice the Christian spiritual disciplines, and dialogue with others on this journey, please join our community online at:
www.owningpoverty.com

---

[8] Merton, Thomas "The Time of the End is the Time of No Room" in *Raids on the Unspeakable* (New Directions, 1966).

Made in the USA
Monee, IL
16 August 2021